Pena
Palace

Pena Palace

PAULO PEREIRA   JOSÉ MARTINS CARNEIRO

MINISTÉRIO DA CULTURA

INSTITUTO
PORTUGUÊS DO
PATRIMÓNIO
ARQUITECTÓNICO

SCALA PUBLISHERS

Contents

ACKNOWLEDGEMENTS

At IPPAR, Instituto Português do Património Arquitectónico, the authors wish to express their thanks to Dulce de Freitas Ferraz, who was in charge or organizing the photographic operation and of collecting the related information and captions, to Isabel Melo, Head of the Commercial Division and to Isabel Lage for her support in co-ordinating this publication.

The authors also wish to express their gratitude to all the people running the Pena National Palace, and to the people in charge of the institutions which are trustees of the works of art related to the Pena Palace who have given permission for their reproduction in this book.

© Instituto Português do Património Arquitectónico (IPPAR) and Scala Publishers, 1999

First published in 1999 by Scala Publishers Ltd
143-149 Great Portland Street
London W1N 45FB

Designed by Peter Ling
Translated by Gilla Evans
Edited by Tim Ayers
Revision to text by A. Miguel Saraiva and John Gilbert
Printed and bound in Spain by Fournier A. Graficas S.A.

Front jacket illustration: General view of the Chapel building, from the Pátio dos Arcos
Back jacket illustration: Aerial view of the Pena National Palace

ISBN 1 85759 175 5 (hardback)
ISBN 972-8087-62-4 (paperback)

PHOTOGRAPHIC CREDITS:

IPPAR/Luís Pavão: pp. 2, 5 , 10, 12, 14, 15, 25, 37, 39, 40, 42, 44, 46, 48, 49, 50, 51, 52, 53, 54, 55, 56, 57, 58, 59, 60, 61, 62, 63, 64, 65, 66, 67, 68, 69, 70, 71, 72, 73, 74, 76, 77, 78, 79, 80, 81, 82, 84, 87, 88, 89, 90, 91, 92, 93, 94, 95, 96, 97, 98, 99, 100, 101, 102, 103, 104, 106, 107, 108, 110, 111, 112, 113, 114, 116, 117, 118, 119, 120, 121, 122
IPPAR/Henrique Ruas: pp. 13, 18, 19, 21, 22, 26, 29, 33, 34, 35, 36, 41, 43, 45, 47, 54, 61, 80, 85, 100, 104, 105, 109, 113, 115, 119
IPPAR/Delfim Ferreira: pp. 27, 78, 84, 93, 97, 100, 103, 111, 118
Biblioteca Nacional/Laura Guerreiro: pp. 16, 20, 111
IPPAR/Manuel Palma: pp. 24, 30
Divisão de Documentação Fotográfica-IPM/Arnaldo Soares: p. 28
Divisão de Documentação Fotográfica-IPM/Henrique Ruas: p. 125
Granja: pp. 26, 98
Photographic Archive of the C. M. L.: pp. 123, 124

Foreword

The Pena National Palace is one of Portugal's most symbolic monuments. A pioneer in Europe of the architectural forms that were to be developed by Romantic sensibility, this palace is a splendid repository of eras and tastes, combined and reconstituted at the behest of a man to whom Portugal's heritage owes a great deal: Dom Fernando II.

As a matter of fact, Dom Fernando II – who came to be known as the Artist-King – as well as a collector, designer and ceramicist, took a greater interest than almost anyone in the architectural legacy he found in Portugal, promoting and sponsoring conservation and restoration work on the most important Portuguese monuments. Pena Palace is also itself, in some ways, a homage to this heritage from different eras, combining in a labyrinthine and multifaceted and occasionally enigmatic space, an impressive range of morphological allusions, from gothic to rocaille, passing through the exotic styles which, at the time, enchanted all those who were fighting for the aesthetic revival of Romanticism. And this is something we find, albeit by contrast, in the interior spaces of the palace, characterized by an exceptional intimacy.

This book is therefore, we believe, a rigorous yet accessible way of conveying this reality, giving Pena Palace and the inspirational Serra de Sintra their rightful place in the history of European architecture and culture.

LUÍS FERREIRA CALADO
President of Instituto Português
do Património Arquitectónico

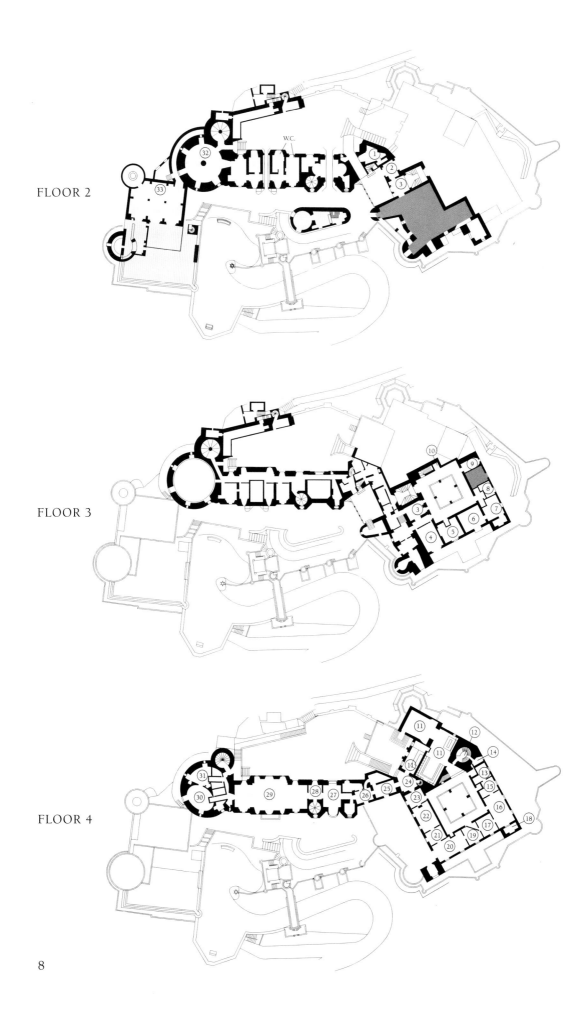

FLOOR 2

FLOOR 3

FLOOR 4

8

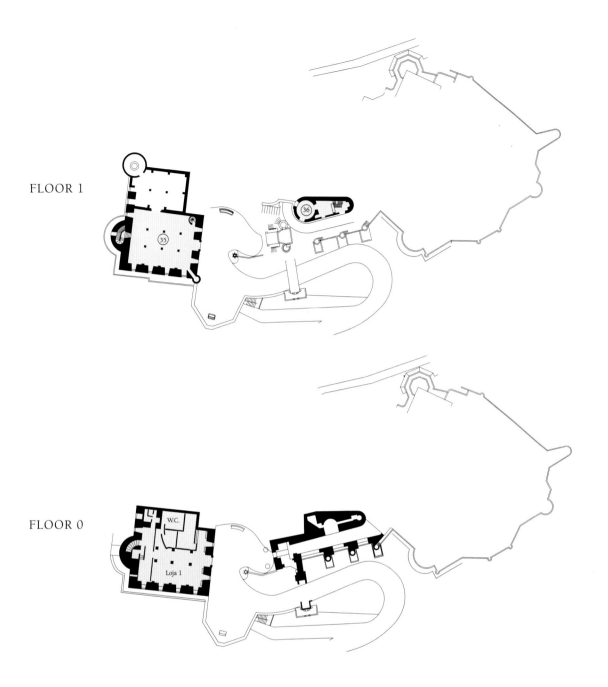

FLOOR 1

FLOOR 0

1 Cloakroom	13 Ladies-in-Waiting's First Room	25 First Hallway
2 Entrance Hall	14 Bathrooms	26 Second Hallway
3 Pantry	15 Ladies-in-Waiting's Second Room	27 Indian Room
4 Dining Room	16 Queen's Bed-Chamber	28 Reception Hall
5 Bedroom	17 Queen's Dressing-Room	29 Noble Hall
6 D. Carlos's Studio	18 Queen's Bathroom	30 D. Manuel II's Quarters
7 D. Carlos's Bedroom	19 Sewing Room	31 D. Manuel II's Quarters/Saxe Room
8 Shower and Massage Room	20 Royal Family's Private Sitting Room	32 Deer Hall
9 Monks' Cell	21 Queen's Boudoir	33 Palace Kitchens
10 St Jerome's Chapel	22 Arab Room	34 Cafetaria
11 Chapel and Sacristy	23 Green Room	35 Restaurant
12 Staircase to the Tower	24 Atrium of the Queen's Terrace	36 Palace Shop 2

Sintra

Pena Palace, founded by Fernando II (1816–1885), stands on one of the peaks of the Serra de Sintra, the major mountain range that lies immediately to the north of Lisbon.

The region dominated by this imposing mountain range has been well populated since prehistoric times and is rich in myths. The megalithic monuments of the mountains (such as the so-called '*tholos* do Monge') and the surrounding area (Belas, Agualva, Carcavelos, Carenque, Praia das Maçãs, Odrinhas, Barreiras, Alto da Vigia), and the archeological remains that have been unearthed, as well as tell-tale place names, reveal that this has long been a sacred place. To geographers of antiquity this was the *mons sacer* or 'sacred mountain' and, to Ptolemy, the 'mountain of the moon'. The Serra de Sintra was a physical and religious pole of reference for this fertile rural region – the region of the Mozarabs – who inclined towards the celebration of its horizons: that of the land with the sky and of the land with the sea.

In the tenth century AD, the geographer Al-Bacr gave an account of the opulence of the region and of its charms: '[Sintra] is one of the towns which depend on Lisbon in the realm of Andaluz, close to the sea. It is permanently enveloped in a mist which never dissipates. Its climate is healthy and the inhabitants long-lived. It has two castles of extreme solidity. The town lies nearly a mile from the sea and serves to irrigate the vegetable plots... The region of Sintra is one of those areas where apples are quite plentiful. These fruits grow to such a size that some reach four spans in circumference. So it is with the pears. Wild violets grow on the Serra de Sintra. Fine amber is extracted from the nearby coast.' In this description an objective portrait of the region is coupled with what amounts to a mythicization of its productive capacities.

In tales of chivalry, these places became overlaid with legends of giants, which appear to be the romantic embodiment of an extraordinary local folklore. The mythical castle of 'Colir' (which can be interpreted as present-day Colares) was situated close to another castle, that of 'Cintra', guarded by a giant, 'o forte Morbanfo', a terrible monster and taker of sacrifices. The heroic knight Clarimundo, father of the Portuguese nation – as told by João de Barros in his *Crónica do Emperador Clarimundo*, 1521 – defeated the giant with arms he had taken from some merchants 'who landed there, sent by the Giant Madorca, sister of Calarna, to her nephew Pantafasul'. Clarimundo then climbed to the top of the tower of the castle of Colir, where his companion and guide, the wise Fanimor, prophesied the 'future' of Portugal in epic verses, when 'the light of the Moon was at its fullest'. Surrounded by the 'singing of Nightingales', dressed in 'long linen robes like those of a priest which he wore underneath, and with a hood on his head, seized by a divine spirit, which fired him with such fury that at times he seemed a Giant... looking now to the East, now to the West, and making the sign of the Cross in all directions', in what sounds like an almost druidical ceremony.

The importance of the Serra de Sintra was later confirmed when the Portuguese court established a temporary residence there, in the Paço da Vila.

Pena Palace and Park

Aerial view of the Pena National Palace

The palace of Sintra is a very old building, which underwent major remodelling from the reign of João I (1357–1433) until the sixteenth century. Its expansion was an organic process that led to an apparently disorderly complex of structures. The first major construction work dates from the beginning of the fifteenth century and the supervision of it is attributed to João Garcia de Toledo, a master mason of Spanish origin, with a particular regard for the Mudejar or Moorish style of building. The so-called 'central structure' of the palace dates from around this period, as do the chapel and the extraordinary kitchen, with its two enormous conical chimneys. Traces of an earlier Moslem residence of the *Wallis* of Chão de Oliva can be seen in the old names such as the Terreiro de Meca (Terrace of Mecca); but also in the organizational logic of the spaces, which derives to a large extent from

Islamic living patterns and social arrangements, with their different levels, small internal courtyards, fountains and pools, in an irregular assortment of buildings giving countless nooks and spaces for recreation and shade. The Sala dos Árabes is one of the oldest rooms, tiled with fifteenth-century *azulejos* (glazed tiles) from Seville, and with a sixteenth-century marble fountain, surmounted by the figure of Proteus, crowning the central jet of water.

The Royal Chapel was partly rebuilt in the Manueline period, retaining its fresco wall decoration, with repeated depictions of the dove of the Holy Spirit, and its carved ceiling, a typically Mudejar ceiling of 'stars' and 'knots'.

In 1505, King Manuel I (1469–1521) decided to improve the palace, giving it a hybrid character, resulting from the combination of a Moorish style with Gothic or 'modern' additions. He called upon the services of a brilliant group of master masons, among them Boytac, whose intervention is documented in 1507, supplying carved capitals for the building. The monarch's chambers were in the east wing and included the great hall, with its Manueline windows, radiating a potent hyperrealist language, in their extraordinary carved ornament of tree-trunks, varied flora and vegetation. This is in a part which links with the internal courtyards, notably the Pátio dos Cisnes – with its central pool – surrounded by mullioned doors and windows, decorated by an *alfiz*, with marble columns and capitals in the shape of 'turbans', in a clear Andalusian allusion. This evocation of Arab buildings was accentuated by the *azulejos*, or tiles, which were brought from Seville to line the various rooms.

The exoticism of the Paço da Vila's architecture is remarkable, even where the Moorish legacy is merely 'copied': the idea being to establish a precocious flavour of 'revival', which was assumed as a courtly fashion.

The pleasant climate of Sintra allied with its proximity to the court made the Serra a favoured resort of the Portuguese aristocracy, especially in the Manueline period and, later, during the reign of João III (1502–57). The majority of the palaces and older estates of the region date from this period: such as the Quinta da Ribafria of the Governor Gaspar Gonçalves; the Quinta da Penha Verde of João de Castro and, later, the Quinta da Nossa Senhora dos Enfermos of Francisco de Holanda, among many others. From this time, the Serra began to be celebrated as a special *locus amoenus*.

In 1539, Gil Vicente, in his *Auto do Inferno*, called Sintra 'an earthly garden of paradise/Sent here by

View of the town of Sintra and the Royal Palace

Armorial Room of the Royal Palace of Sintra

Solomon/For a king of Portugal'. A place of *soirées*, literary discussions, tournaments and theatrical performances, the Renaissance was to give the palace a renown that it has never lost. The poet Luísa Sigeia celebrated it in 1546: 'By the western banks of the river, where the Sun, as night draws near, approaches the ocean, and borne in his ivory carriage, almost touches the immense sea, his horses tired from their long run, lies a place where a pleasant valley, between sheer rocks rising to the skies, curves between gracious hills filled with the sound of murmuring streams'.

THE EARLY ROMANTICS AND 'GLORIOUS EDEN'

For its beautiful setting, the Romantics made Sintra a place of compulsory pilgrimage – one of the most important, if not perhaps one of the first, in their cultural geography. They appropriated it to such an extent that Southey had no hesitation in asserting, with undisguised arrogance, that 'Cintra is too good a place for the Portuguese; it is only fit for us Goths, for Germans or English...'

The poet Almeida Garrett celebrated Sintra, recalling in his verses the successive paradoxes arising from the enjoyment of nature to be felt there: 'Oh cold grottoes/Oh sighing fountains, oh breaths/Of the enamoured woods, gentle pastures,/Green hills, gigantic ridges', echoing the sentiments of William Beckford or Lord Byron, who referred to it as a 'Glorious Eden'. Byron praised the profusion of this place, which, according to him, was nothing less than 'the most delightful in Europe' and celebrated its unique potential in the province of this new feeling for beauty, which was then coming to the fore. In this he was followed by draughtsmen and engravers, such as William Burnett, Clémentine Brélaz, Domenico Schiopetta and Colebrook Stockdale: 'There is a pleasure in the pathless woods,/There is a rapture on the lonely shore,/There is a society, where none intrudes,/By the deep Sea, and music in its roar:/ I love not Man the less, but Nature more' (Lord Byron, *Childe Harold's Pilgrimage*). He expressed that 'atmospheric' quality, with all its phenomenological scope, which attracted poets and lovers of ideal evocations of paradise. At Sintra, a place 'more for dreaming than describing', according to Dorothy Wordsworth, the imaginary world took on a new form. The Serra recovered, in short, its symbolic and mythic value, as Richard Strauss asserted, when gazing at the then-completed Pena Palace, speaking of the 'castle of the Holy Grail' perched over the 'true garden of Klingsor'.

Pena Park. Ferns

The Pena Monastery

According to tradition, the Pena area became a place of Christian devotion at an early date, after the miraculous appearance of Our Lady on a rock. Some historians refer to the existence of a small grotto or chapel nearby from at least the twelfth century. Documents record that in the time of João I the priests of the neighbouring church of São Pedro de Penaferrim (São Pedro de Sintra) held mass there on Saturdays. But only with Garcia de Resende is the visit recorded of João II and Queen Leonor, on a pilgrimage to this holy spot, in the year 1493.

We do know that it was very difficult to reach, because of its situation and the harsh rocky environment. It was left to Manuel I to create a broader and less confined setting, enabling a monastery to be built of timber next to the already existing little chapel, to give thanks for the voyage of Vasco da Gama to India in 1502. It is said that, on a visit to this place, the king had spotted the returning Portuguese fleet in the distance, still at sea but about to enter the River Tagus. Because of the growing importance of the Order of Saint Jerome during the time of King Manuel, the monastery of Nossa Senhora da Pena was later given by the king to this Order, which had been in residence at Penha Longa, also in the Sintra region, since 1355. The spirit of this hermitic and contemplative Order was well suited to the spartan location.

Cloister of the Pena Monastery before the nineteenth-century restoration work.
Watercolour by G. Vivian, lithographed by Louis Hague, 1839
(National Library)

The construction of a new monastery was decided upon by King Manuel around 1511, this time from stone and masonry, because of the fragility of wood and its rapid deterioration. Chroniclers and historians at the beginning of the nineteenth century attributed its design to an (imaginary) architect of Italian origin, one João Potassi, who designed it as 'a church, cloister, dormitory, offices, belfry, etc. all with a rib vaulted roof, one being of rock and the other of stone from Ançã, with the full excellence of art and architecture, in the style of the period, to serve as a memorial, since this was the place where His Highness had caught sight of the fleet, and as a sacred Monument to show the generations to come the now well proven daring and courage of the Lusitanians across the seas at the beginning of the sixteenth century' (Abbot de Castro e

Sousa). The passage reveals three important facts: the traditional attribution of all highly esteemed work to 'Italians', a typical pre-Romantic attitude; the need to provide the monastery with lasting structures in keeping with the demands of the rule of the Order; and the association of the Pena with the 'discoveries' and the seafaring exploits of the Portuguese. Contemporary sources leave no room for doubt, however. The person in charge of the construction was the master mason Diogo Boytac (the 'João Potassi' of the chronicles being no more than an Italianate corruption of this name), who was then working in Sintra on various royal projects, and the Late Gothic and Moorish vocabulary of the building are confirmation of this.

Around 1513 the new building was complete, and nineteen monks came to inhabit it. Even so, and in spite of the considerable improvement resulting from this building work, the Jeronymite friar Brother Heitor Pinto still commented in his *Diálogos* (in the 1560s) that the 'Monastery because of its astonishing elevation seems more like an eagle's nest than a dwelling for monks'.

ABANDONMENT

Although gradually declining in importance, whether because it was slowly forgotten, or because the income of the Order was failing, the Pena Monastery remained occupied and active until at least 1743, when lightning damaged the bell tower and several wings of the building. The great earthquake of 1755, which devastated Lisbon and its surrounding area, also inflicted serious damage on the monastery, leaving just half a dozen rooms and the chapel. Only four or five monks remained in occupation. From a document dated 1828 we learn that the monastery was still inhabited, but by just one monk and a lay person. In its condition, the Pena Monastery was not very different from many other small buildings of the same type, perched on the peaks of the Serra de Sintra – 'the Horrid crags, by toppling convent crown'd', as Byron described them. They celebrated this mythical place and christianized it. The

Pena was distinguished by its greater expressiveness, however, resulting from the building projects of Dom Manuel's time.

The promulgation between 1833 and 1834 by the Portuguese liberal government of laws dissolving the religious orders led to the suppression of the monastery. On 6 May 1834, King Pedro IV ordered an inventory to be made of the secular effects of the house, leaving only the church open to worship, still furnished with its images and 'ornaments'. After that, it was abandoned until the reign of King Fernando II.

A drawing by Casanova gives us a view of the building before the major renovation carried out by Fernando II. The angle from which the view was taken deliberately accentuates the monastery's inaccessibility, showing in the foreground the zigzag road that leads up to it. Above, the huge bulk of the monastery stands out to the right, with the tower behind, with a sixteenth-century roof built over it to replace what must have been a Manueline turret, which had collapsed. From that time on, the other buildings add a sense of

Pátio das hospedarias (Lodging House courtyard) and chapel entrance before Dom Fernando II's revivalist and restoration work, showing the primitive bell tower. Watercolour by G. Vivian, lithographed by Louis Hague, 1839 (National Library)

monumentality to a complex of small dimensions, using the effect of its unexpected situation.

A watercolour by G. Vivian gives us a closer view. He portrays the entrance courtyard of the chapel – today the great North Terrace. In the foreground, we see the top of the former lodging house, crowned by typically Manueline battlements. This structure was later demolished to make room for the New Palace. The rest of the building shows the enormous weathering, caused by age and the early years of abandonment, which it had already suffered when the pictures were produced. The chapel entrance is marked out by the porch, surmounted by a pyramid-shaped turret, also

Manueline in style, covered on the outside with chequered tiles, which were retained during the renovation by Dom Fernando II. Another watercolour by the same artist shows the cloister of the monastery, which was retained with very few alterations.

Less precise, but valuable as evidence of the impression made on the king himself by the little monastery, is a drawing signed by him and transposed into an engraving in 1839. This picture, which may have been done from memory, records the general appearance and location of the buildings, reduced to a minimum on the top of the Sintra rocks. In the foreground is a shepherd with his goats, whom we shall be meeting again... Of the same date is a plan drawn by Nicolau Pires, made after the building was bought by the monarch, at his request. At first-floor level, around the quadrangular cloister, the structure has fourteen rooms or cells. The tower is arranged at an oblique angle, with the respective spiral staircase and the group of buildings formed by the choir, chapel and sacristy. Annexed to this is the small rectangle of the lodgings. At a distance, lie the stables.

In September 1834 the auction of the monastery's effects was begun, as well as the offer for rent of the 'Enclosure and Buildings of the said former Monastery'. As no one took up the offer, it was decided that the property should be sold by public auction. On 26 September 1838, the Government Journal published a list of various properties for auction. One lot was identified as 'Monastery of Nossa Senhora da Pena, on the Serra de Cintra... and other attached lodgings, and the surrounding land, which consists of a lemon grove, fields, pine grove and scrubland', at an auction price of 700,000 réis. The Official Journal cautioned that the purchase was to be made 'with the express clause that the bidder is obliged to ensure its proper conservation... as it is a national monument, and as the Church contains a finely sculptured retable'.

Drawn by the natural beauty of Sintra and deeply appreciative – now in a romantic vein – of the barren and wild aesthetic of the mountains and its countless ruins, Dom Fernando decided to buy it and delegated his agent to purchase the monastery for the stated price. This was done on 3 November 1838 before the Public Finance Board.

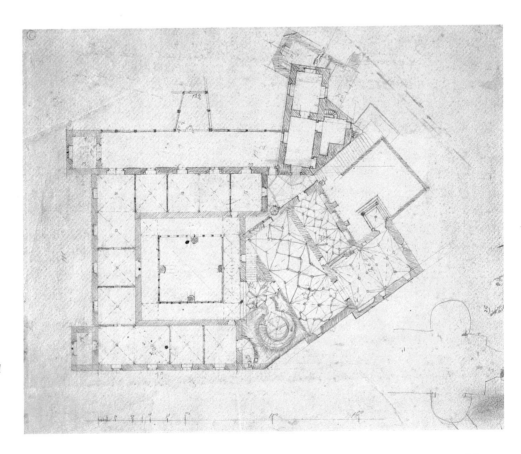

Plan of the Pena Monastery before the restoration work. Pencil drawing by Nicolau Pires, undated (1839?) (Pena National Palace collection)

Fernando II

Dom Fernando II, or Fernando Augusto Francisco António Kohary de Saxe Coburg-Gotha, to give him his full name, was the second husband of the Queen of Portugal, Dona Maria II. He was born in Vienna on 29 October 1816, the first son of Duke Fernando Jorge Augusto (1785–1851) and Antoinette Gabrielle, Princess of Kohary (1797–1862).

Appointed Fernando's tutor, it was the theologian Carl Dietz who guided the upbringing and education of the prince, accompanying him to Portugal in 1836. He was among the nobles and friends who, in January 1836, boarded the warship HMS *Manchester* of the English fleet, on a voyage that would take Fernando to Brussels, Paris and London, arriving finally at Lisbon on 8 April 1836. He was just 19 years old.

Dietz prepared for the young prince a complete plan of study in various disciplines in the fields of the sciences and liberal arts. Of these, the young pupil absorbed with particular interest the direct observation of nature, to which his regular stays at the castle of Rosenau, the family's country residence near Coburg, certainly contributed. However, he took up all the arts with eagerness, with special emphasis on drawing and music. Influenced from childhood by the propitious ambience of the city of Vienna, where a pleasant cosmopolitan atmosphere held sway, he would become an inveterate music lover, and remained for his whole life a keen amateur musician, attending and putting on concerts, musical entertainments and operas. The waltzes of Johann Strauss, the 'Lieder' of Schubert and the compositions of Liszt, who, to Dom Fernando's great joy, visited Lisbon in 1845, all formed the backdrop of the young aristocrat's education. The position of the Coburgs and the wealth of his mother's family, whose inheritance was dispersed around Austria and especially in Hungary, enabled Dom Fernando and his parents to lead a life of ease and culture.

D. Fernando II quando jovem
(*Dom Fernando II as a young man*).
Oil on canvas, c. 1836
(*Ajuda National Palace collection*)

D. Maria II quando jovem (*Dona Maria II
as a young woman*). *Oil on canvas, c. 1834*
(*Ajuda National Palace collection*)

Portugal was being torn apart by civil war, from which Liberalism would emerge the winner. As a result, this young prince, the representative of a constitutional monarchy, emerged as a serious contender for the second marriage of Dona Maria II, who, at the age of 17, was already the widow of Dom Augusto de Leuchtenberg (1810–1835), with no issue from this first union. The second marriage was of major political importance in maintaining the Liberal position, as the Queen herself was the symbol of Constitutionalism. The entire court aspired to stability in the country and there was an urgent need to ensure royal descendants.

The marriage (or rather, the ceremony to ratify the marriage, since it had already taken place by correspondence on 1 January 1836) was held in Lisbon cathedral on 9 April 1836. When the queen gave birth to Prince Pedro, the future King Pedro V, in 1837, the prince consort was immediately given the title of King Fernando II. He gradually became integrated in Portuguese society, and in October he was appointed commander-in-chief of the Army, a post which he filled with undisguised discomfort and a degree of ineptitude. Not cut out for military life, his lack of interest and somewhat naïve attitude led him to face unexpected aggravations. The Marquis of Fronteira records the following episode in his memoirs: 'We saw His Majesty arriving at the Arsenal, with the intention of going over to the Cacilhas side of the river. He had informed us that he was crossing the Tagus in order to review the forces of General Vinhaes. A few hours later, I received some

mail from Marshal Saldanha, which included a letter for her Majesty the Queen. We tried to inform the king of the letter and it was decided that the general adjutant should go and tell him. He crossed the Tagus and, although he was expecting to find the king at the positions close to Setúbal, he found him in the sitting room of the navy accountant, on Calçada de Almada, singing the duet of Semiramis with the daughter of the household. The letter from the marshal did not compel His Majesty to end the concert...'

In 1851 the country was agitated by the Regeneration movement. Marshal Saldanha led an uprising and set up the Junta do Porto, preparing to march on Lisbon. The crown needed to respond with military might. However, lingering in Santarém, the commander-in-chief delayed the arrival of his troops at Coimbra, where it was supposed he would obstruct the passage of the dissidents. Once in Coimbra, he opted, against all military rules (and those of etiquette, which were also important...), to hold a dialogue with the insurgents, subjecting himself to a daily humiliation when he received representation from the academic body of the University. In the acid words of the Marquis of Fronteira, 'they began by asking him to resign from the Ministry; given this, they congratulated him. They congratulated him on the revolt of Porto; they congratulated him on the entry of the Duke of Saldanha; they practically congratulated him on the abdication of his noble Wife, which was about to occur'. Finally, he ordered his troops to withdraw and they returned to

The Countess of Edla's chalet

Lisbon, against all government resolutions and the will of his wife, this being perhaps the only matter on which they disagreed.

It is true that there were no violent clashes and his benevolent pacifism – called cowardice by some – may reflect his awareness of the suffering in a country recently immersed in a tumultuous civil war, while also reflecting a personality educated to value culture and science over arms and political *praxis*. Putting up with the joking, and accusations of weakness of spirit and lack of discernment with which, justly or unjustly, he was greeted in Lisbon, Dom Fernando's difficult military career came to an end – probably to his great relief.

However, the birth of heirs within the Portuguese royal family cemented what everyone recognized to be a benevolent union between the young couple, who from the start showed a strong mutual affection. In the seventeen years that Dona Maria II and Dom Fernando were married, during which time the queen became

Left: D. Fernando II, *portrait by Layraud,*
oil on canvas, 1877
(Pena National Palace collection)

Dom Fernando II, *marble medallion*
by the Countess of Edla, 1874

Left: O Rei D. Fernando II vestido à cruzado (*King Fernando II dressed as a crusader*), photograph by Wenceslau Cifka, c. 1879
(Library of the Ducal Palace of Vila Viçosa)

Below: Engraving by Dom Fernando II

Bottom: D. Fernando II intitulando-se Barão de Avis (*Dom Fernando II styling himself as Baron of Avis*). Engraving by Dom Fernando II, 1870 (private collection). An interesting iconographic item showing the 'Artist-King' himself parodying his taste for collecting and bric-a-brac

Fruit bowl, Qing Dynasty, end of eighteenth century (Pena National Palace collection)

pregnant eleven times, mutual respect and a sincere family union prevailed: so much so that the queen, in spite of his successive political and military failures, 'made no comment and would allow no comment to be made', according to the Marquis of Fronteira, one of the king's sharpest critics, as we have seen. The queen died on 15 November 1853, however, giving birth to their eleventh child, who did not survive either.

MARRIAGE TO THE COUNTESS OF EDLA

Dom Fernando's second marriage, to the Countess of Edla, was certainly also significant for the political context of the time. The great fondness of the monarch for music and singing meant that the most important social event in Lisbon was the opening of the well attended opera season at the São Carlos Theatre. The lyric singer Elisa Hensler came to perform in 1860, in the role of page in Verdi's *Ballo in Masquere*. Seven

Wall fountain in the shape of a peacock, Companhia das Índias, 2nd half of eighteenth century (Pena National Palace collection)

years after he became a widower, Dom Fernando met Elisa and a strong intimate relationship formed between them.

The king became the butt of a great deal of criticism, since, in the eyes of many, Elisa was a mere singer. The contemporary press lambasted him unmercifully. But nothing was going to prevent Dom Fernando II from marrying Miss Hensler (1826–1929), if only morganatically. Already before the marriage, in fact, the singer had received from Dom Fernando's cousin, Duke Ernest II of Saxony, the title of Countess of Edla. The union itself took place on 10 February 1869, at the Quinta de Benfica, owned by the Princess Isabel Maria, the aunt of Dona Maria II.

Until the king's death, the couple were extremely happy, by all accounts. The monarch always treated his second wife with affection and had the so-called Casa do Regalo, better known as the 'Chalet da Condessa', built for her in Pena Park. This became their favourite retreat and the house still stands as a memorial to a life whose end would be viewed with unquestionable affection by the Portuguese, since she never called into question the special relationship that Dom Fernando had with his kingdom. Instead she closed the existential circle, linking the monarch with artistic creation, bringing it into his own sphere of intimacy.

AN ARTISTIC PERSONALITY AND PATRON OF THE ARTS

The education of Dom Fernando awoke in him a truly contemporary artistic personality. He was an amateur painter and became known as the *rei-artista*

(artist-king), a title coined in 1841 by the writer António Feliciano de Castilho. Fernando began at the age of 19 to produce engravings and then extended his work to modelling, drawing and painting.

Although they cannot be seen as the manifestation of an exceptional talent, the engravings and drawings focused on small things, or on myths crystallized in quasi-legendary characters, establishing a break between the tradition which served as his starting point, and which he studied from the collection that he had been putting together since he was a child (Dürer, Holbein, Cranach, Rembrandt – who fascinated him particularly – Rubens, Piranesi and many others), and the principles of a new artistic movement, decidedly Romantic in vein. Those who were accustomed to the 'old order' saw Dom Fernando's technical limitations almost exclusively; but those who were aware of the new artistic realities emerging across Europe – amongst them Count Raczynsky, who otherwise had a sharp critical spirit – recognized the merit of the artist-king's work. It is not without merit, even if is not in any way in the vanguard. And it has a particular authorial mark, when the value of his application to

Above: Cinco Artistas em Sintra (Five Artists in Sintra), by Cristino da Silva, oil on canvas, signed and dated, 1855 (Chiado Museum)

Right: Dishes mounted in the form of a round table, Imari porcelain, Japan, seventeenth – eighteenth century (Pena National Palace collection)

ceramics is recognized, a field that Dom Fernando explored, for example, at the factory of Sacavém, where he was a frequent visitor.

His taste as a collector reveals an eminently eclectic tendency, which, for this very reason, can be identified with Romanticism. He collected everything, but with a particular fondness for ceramics (from Italian majolica to the fine glazed earthenware produced by the Rato factory) and porcelain – Meissen, Wedgwood, Haviland, Capo di Monte, Copeland, Crown Derby – which he acquired to the point of mania.

Dom Fernando II, c. 1875.
Oil on canvas by Miguel Lupi
(Mafra National Palace
collection)

Along with the queen, he was patron of the Academia Real de Belas-Artes, founded in 1836. He supported the purchase of eighty-three paintings, which would form the basis of the collection of the Galeria Nacional de Pintura. A significant part of this collection was housed in what is now the Museu Nacional de Arte Antiga.

At the same time, he encouraged development of the arts by offering study bursaries to young painters and sculptors, buying or borrowing many of their works with the aim of promoting them. Cristino da

Silva, Tomás da Anunciação (one of his favourite artists), Visconde de Meneses (who benefited from a royal bursary in Rome), Francisco José Resende, António Patrício, Francisco Metrass, Silva Porto, Columbano and Rafael Bordalo Pinheiro, Leonel Marques Pereira, João Vaz, Simões de Almeida and Vítor Bastos all owed a great deal to the direct support and patronage of the king.

Among the works of these artists, the painting *Cinco Artistas em Sintra* (Five Artists in Sintra), painted in 1855, became a veritable emblem of Portuguese

Romanticism. An old shepherd and a country girl, who is minding four curious urchins, are leaning over Tomás da Anunciação, who is seated and working, with a sketchbook open on his lap. Behind is the painter Metrass; in the background can be seen Vítor Bastos, José Rodrigues and Cristino da Silva. In this spontaneous self-portrait of a group united by the same – and new – pleasure, the Serra de Sintra itself has a significant presence, the rocky hill serving as background to the scene (looking like an intriguing megalith); and to the left, at the top of the mountain, painted in muted colours appears the old – and new – Pena Palace.

Fernando was also the patron, from 1864, of the Real Associação dos Architectos Civis e Archeologos Portuguezes and he sponsored, as chairman of its committee of honour, the 'Retrospective Exhibition of Portuguese and Spanish Ornamental Art' at the South Kensington Museum in London, an exhibition of major importance for the recognition of Portuguese artistic trends and for their internationalization.

CONSERVATION OF THE HERITAGE

Through Fernando's mediation, the first campaign to restore national monuments worthy of the name was carried out in Portugal. An enthusiast for architecture, as can be seen, he began visiting national monuments, after getting to know the Jerónimos Monastery in Belém, which was in any case quite close to one of the royal residences. He was also particularly impressed by the monastery of Batalha, for which, in his own words, he felt 'a kind of fanaticism'. He had certainly known of it in Vienna, since it was published in a remarkable survey by James Murphy, *Plans, Elevations, Sections and Views of the Church of Batalha*, 1795, later translated into German by Engelhard in 1813.

For Dom Fernando, royal interpreter of a cultural context which held the middle ages and its remains in high regard, the monastery of Batalha became a model for the crusade he was about to undertake on behalf of Portuguese monuments. He was occasionally assisted by the inspector-general of public works of the time, Luís Mouzinho de Alburquerque, who in 1854 published *Memoria Inédita Acerca do Edifício Monumental da Batalha*, shortly after being assured of the budgetary funds to start the repair and restoration work. According to Pinto Coelho, we owe to Dom Fernando 'the fact that this magnificent building is still here, because shortly afterwards the government, at the instigation of that royal and vigorous patron of the arts, decreed that several major repairs be undertaken; otherwise the country would have lost this national monument'.

In Alcobaça, he was to gaze with sadness upon the monuments to Dom Pedro and Dona Inês, complaining of the pitiful state into which both they and the building that housed them had fallen. In the Jerónimos Monastery, Dom Fernando was an interested party and he closely monitored the restoration work that was being carried out since it had been left by the religious Order. The improvement of the monument was begun under the direction of the Englishman Colson and, with various ups and downs, continued until the 1870s, being directed at last by a pair of architects and scenographers, Rambois and Cinatti; not without some trouble and polemic, as a result of the collapse of the newly built central tower in 1878. Interest was also taken in the Convento de Cristo at Tomar, which underwent a number of improvements through the direct intervention of the monarch, shortly after the town was elevated to district capital in 1843.

In the long term, evidence of the monarch's intervention – which was not limited to influencing endowments from the state budget, since he himself financed some of the restorations with money from his own pocket – can be seen in the work which was carried on in the second half of the nineteenth century in Lisbon cathedral and the Torre de Belém, and then extending to other areas of the country. But his most significant action, for its symbolic nature, was his rescue of one of the masterpieces of Late Gothic metalwork: the monstrance of Belém. This took place at the Mint, during a visit he was making: upon opening a cupboard, he found the object waiting to be melted down and transformed into coinage...

The Building of Pena Palace

In the period when the construction of the Pena Palace began, an extended debate was beginning in Portugal – in the wake of what was happening and had happened in the rest of Europe – on the subject of national heritage and, especially, its medieval remains. A new mentality in a Romantic vein was gradually absorbing leading thinkers, emphasizing the technical, structural and symbolic value of the Gothic and, as a consequence, disparaging classicism in all its forms.

This apparent conflict found an echo in the positions defended by several critics and historians. Raczynski, author of a *Dictionnaire des artistes portugais*, recorded in his book of essays *Les Arts en Portugal*, 1846, a curious observation which he attributed to the historian Alexandre Herculano: 'I consider ingenious and rather apposite an observation made to me one day by Sr Herculano regarding the architecture of Manuel. It is the endurance of the Gothic style compared with the style of Francis I'. This historicist interpretation of styles was justifiable, especially coming from a rigorous and prestigious historian like Herculano, who was also an active journalist. He promoted the magazine *O Panorama*, which had a

Pena Palace in the final phase of construction. Photograph, Vigé et Pléssix (Ajuda Library collection).
The Serra is barren and rugged without the established vegetation that now forms the scenery of Pena Palace

33

Romantic profile and published in its pages various articles on the subject, among them several by a young Luso-Brazilian, Francisco Adolfo Varnhagen.

Herculano was basically a liberal constitutionalist and a nationalist, almost always regarded as the conscience of the nation. His ideological trajectory, like that of the great poet and prose writer Almeida Garrett, was to be defined during the Civil War, which set the adherents of Liberalism, identified with Prince Pedro, in opposition to the defenders of absolutism, identified with Prince Miguel. With the victory of the Liberals in 1834, ideological progressivism won the day and, with it, nationalist ideas which found in the Portuguese middle ages the best institutional model for governing men in peace and justice, through institutions traditionally considered to be liberating, notably the dividing of the country into 'municipalities', evidence of the municipalist vitality of the middle classes against the supremacy of the nobility.

This somewhat simplistic but nevertheless appealing view of things found sympathy among young people, such as Francisco Adolfo Varnhagen. Varnhagen was born in Brazil in 1816, the same year as Prince Fernando, the son of the geologist and naturalist Friedrich Varnhagen and Maria de Sá Magalhães. Having grown up in Portugal and served in the Portuguese army, loyal to the Liberals, he claimed Brazilian nationality in 1839 in order to express his ideological progressiveness. This helps us to evaluate Varnhagen's role in the aesthetic choices that were made in the Pena Palace.

In his youth, Varnhagen produced a small, but significant *œuvre* on the history of architecture. Among his early works was an article on the Torre de Belém, 1840, and another series that he published later as a small book, entitled *Notícia Histórica e Descritiva do*

Mosteiro de Belém, 1842. At the age of just 26, he presented what may be considered the first text on the modern history of architecture in Portugal, coining for the first time the term 'Manueline', as a neologism to describe the architecture and art of the time of King Manuel I. It was Varnhagen who gave this term, which would have a lasting fortune, its historical and critical content.

What Varnhagen found in the Jerónimos Monastery was the manifestation of the maritime 'discoveries', a material expression of the period of greatest glory and expansionist momentum of the Portuguese nation. He identified in Belém the 'national style' that Portugal lacked, creating it in the true way of the Romantics by giving it a 'name', or inventing it, literally, in epistemological terms: and so 'Manueline' came into being. Very early on the term began to circulate, taking on a prominent role when it spread to the poet Almeida Garrett, who used it a number of times in his writings. It is not surprising, therefore, that the context for the creation (or invention) of Pena

Palace, was a 'Manueline' context – rather nationalistic, rigorously progressive – identified with the dawning of new times and with Liberalism.

The circle from which this name came – and the definition of what it named – was, in any case, a closed circle, which had its own logic and social structure. Almeida Garrett, for example, was a friend of the young Varnhagen and they were neighbours in the Chiado district. The two had adjacent boxes in the Teatro de São Carlos, a special venue for the Romantic intellectual and one attended frequently by Dom Fernando, as we have seen. In his turn, the architect of

Probable visit of Queen Maria II to the Pena construction. Black lithograph, drawn and printed by Legrand (Sintra Town Hall History Archive). In the foreground is the retinue; in the background are the buttresses of the "spiral" tunnel, the new tower and, to the right, the monastery's outbuildings already in their revivalist apparel

Legrand lith.   Lith. de M.L. do C.te R. N. dos M.tos Nº 12 L.

Uma vista exterior do Paço Real de N.S. da Pena, na serra de Cintra.

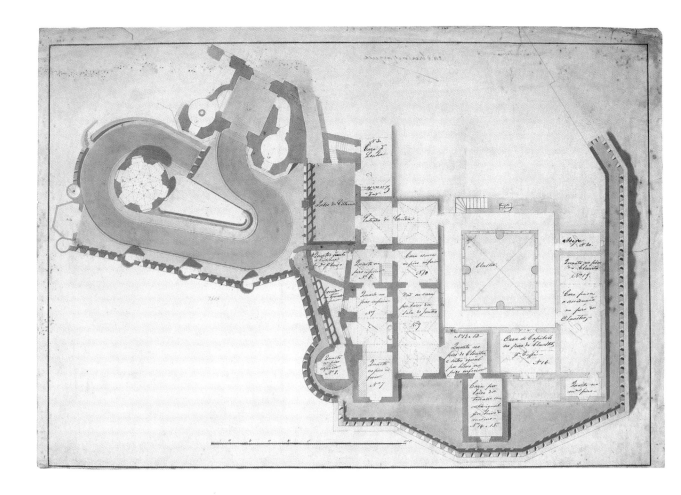

Pena Palace, the Baron von Eschwege, who it is legitimate to suppose had served in the Liberal army alongside Varnhagen, supported the young Luso-Brazilian's entry into the Academy of Sciences. Varnhagen's companionship with Dom Fernando II was also apparently frank and open; and he certainly had access to the king's library. What these men discussed in their comings and goings to nights at the opera is easy to imagine.

An ambience of intellectualism and taste took shape, which was to be reflected in the choices and architectural approach of the Romantic palace. The 'Manueline' corresponded then to an inevitable and necessary 'national' style, reflecting the vibrancy of the Portuguese people and its adventurous spirit at the time of the discoveries (or its *zeitgeist*); the success of which travelled beyond its frontiers through the writing of various authors, amongst them Edgar Quinet – to mention just one among many – giving rise to the association of the style with a maritime pseudo-symbolism, which was to find expression not only in the Pena Palace but also in the refurbishment of the Jerónimos Monastery.

Plan of the area where the Pena Monastery stood, showing the alterations made to the first and second floors, as well as the site of the portico and the turret enclosed by the entrance, unsigned and undated (1842?), pencil drawing with grey and pink watercolour (Pena National Palace collection)

After defining the ten 'formal characteristics' of the Manueline style in his pamphlet, providing the new designation with content, Varnhagen proceeded to make a list of his three preferred architectural styles (1843): 'the Egyptian, the Arab [Moorish] from southern Spain and the Christian-Romantic [*sic*], using this expression (the opposite of the Christian-Classical which still dominates today) to explain the style known as Gothic, its infancy and decadence'. In reality, this stylistic list, with the addition of Manueline, finds its form in the stylistic programme of the Pena Palace, as Eschwege eclectically planned it.

ESCHWEGE,
THE ARCHITECT BARON

Entrada para o Palácio Real da Pena na Serra de Cintra (*Entrance to the Pena Royal Palace on Serra de Sintra*), *lithograph in black printed by C. Legrand, 1843 (Pena National Palace collection)*

The unexpected creator of one of the earliest Romantic mansions of Europe (much earlier than the famous castles of Ludwig II of Bavaria) was the enigmatic Wilhelm Ludwig, Baron von Eschwege, born in Renânia in the province of Hessen-Kassel in 1777 – a curious character, of whom, however, scant memory remains. A naturalist, a student of mineralogy, geology and botany, and a military engineer by profession, he worked in Portugal in the mines of Foz do Alge from 1803. Having joined the Portuguese army as artillery captain from 1807, he fought the invading French troops, and left for Brazil in 1810, where he produced significant work in the field of geology and mining. Having taken on the post of mining director, he was removed by the Miguelistas. Reinstated by the Liberals, he was promoted to brigadier of the army in 1835. Familiar with the customs of the Portuguese, he published *Portugal ein Stat- und Sittengemalde... (Portugal Statistical Moral Picture – Scenes and Sketches...)* in 1833, which was certainly read by Dom Fernando, in spite of being seized by the German authorities before being republished in 1837; and had an influence on the political choices of the young prince. From his familiarity with cultured circles in the capital, the baron was already held in esteem. As for his relationship with Dom Fernando II, it is presumed that this was one of great trust, for the king was to give him

37

carte blanche to design the renovation of the Pena Palace. He took his side against Possidónio da Silva, architect to the royal house at the time, when the first disagreements arose between them, during the implementation of the project.

It is somewhat disconcerting that a military engineer rather than a trained architect should have carried out this important task. But Dom Fernando wanted to make this 'his' palace, to the point of participating in its design. Furthermore, the culture of the Baron von Eschwege, who was on intimate terms with von Humboldt and Goethe on one of his trips round Europe, and certainly familiar with the essays of Schlegel on the excellence of the Gothic and its supposed relationship with nature, would speak more to him than that of a practical (if competent) Portuguese architect. It seems that the 'Germanness' of von Eschwege and his modernity in terms of taste gained the favour of Dom Fernando, who wanted to see the work done without hesitations or needless complications and, above all, under technical conditions that were not the most propitious. As Raczynski wrote of Eschwege, 'L'architecture n'est pas sa spécialité, il s'en occupe en animateur que y est porté par un goût très décidé qui y a fait quelques études et dont l'esprit est très cultivé', but this 'cultivated spirit' and 'taste' made of the Rhineland engineer a personality served by long experience, capable of wilful but consistent management. He was almost 60 when he was 'entrusted with the Management of all the Works of the Pena Palace, and all the responsibility lay with him', as he stated in a protesting letter to his colleague Possidónio, bringing an end to any possible disputes.

PROGRESS OF CONSTRUCTION

We can deduce from the surviving original plans and documentation for the Pena project that von Eschwege surrounded himself with assistants to meet any technical needs. So we see emerging, involved in the design and building of the palace, Nicolau Pires, who drew up plans, if he did not help him in the preparation of the magnificent elevations; and the master stonemason João Henriques, 'one of the most skilled artists of this Kingdom', who was the Baron's assistant. Upon him lay the task of 'supervising the construction work', which he did with evident efficiency, staying to administer the plan of works that the German engineer

entrusted to him when he was temporarily away in Germany in 1847. The former was to take charge of the surveying, drawings and technical details of the project, in which he had acquired practice on other royal projects; the latter, of supervising the civil engineering work and co-ordinating the construction site – to which, curiously, Varnhagen says he paid a visit in order to gather some of the 'technical terms' to include in the glossary of his little book.

In terms of inspiration or antecedents, Baron von Eschwege was familiar with the palace of Stolzenfels (designed by Schinkel and Schnitzel, built between 1834 and 1835), the castle of Rheinstein (designed by Lassaulx, built around 1824) and the palace of Babelsberg, which is a possible model for the layout of the Pena Palace, being similar in dimensions and spacial organization (José Teixeira). In addition, various publications were available in Europe showing British mansions, mostly neo-Gothic in style, but some also notable for the orientalist exoticism that was coming into fashion. The baron, who was to visit North Africa, was not untouched by the fascination of Islamic architecture; and, very close to the Pena Palace, the Palácio da Vila itself served as a reference point for a medieval style of architecture, with Moorish influences, most particularly in its unusual tiled wall coverings, in a note of originality that was entirely Portuguese. Even so, the aesthetic decision made by the baron is intriguing, because, in spite of these examples, the building of the Pena Palace emerges from the void, combining a range of eclectic notes, and forming a new starting point.

The progress of work was initially quite rapid. If Dom Fernando intended initially just to rebuild or renovate the old monastery, he soon became convinced that these improvements would not be sufficient to guarantee the degree of comfort and dignity required of a royal residence. This change of strategy must have come about around the beginning of 1840. By this time, von Eschwege had rebuilt the access to the building via a paved road with a pronounced curve, a novelty for the period, and had ordered the building of the famous tunnel which served simultaneously as a support and as a covering over part of the route (inaccurately described as a 'spiral'), preceded by a neo-medieval portico flanked by two polygonal towers (to which a drawbridge was later added). Completed in

View of the buttresses of the access tunnel

38

Above: Prospecto do Palacio a Castellado da Pena do Lado d (*View of the Fortified Palace from the right), unsigned and undated (1842?), Indian ink and grey watercolour on paper (Pena National Palace collection). Building plan: The drawing shows in the foreground and to the centre, the façade of the sloping tunnel. To the right, the monastery building dominated by the Clock Tower; no significant changes can be seen here in relation to what was actually carried out, apart from the appearance of some aspects of the finish. To the left, below, the service building, accommodating coach-houses and kitchens, shown at an angle, appears much as it does today, but is simplified in this drawing (the final version was enhanced by "Indian" windows). The extensive building added to the great cylindrical tower is what documents later refer to as the "New Palace", resulting from the decision to extend the building with a new construction. This also shows few structural changes. In reality, the vertical effect was slightly reduced as all the visible chimneys were eliminated; at the same time the semi-spherical tower of the stairs was taken from the main façade and moved to the inside of the monument*

Left: Interior view of the access tunnel

1840, the elevations of these structures, with their circular buttresses and their battlemented corona, altered the image presented by the ancient monument, in their monumentality and spacial expressiveness particularly, and certainly had an effect on Dom Fernando, who conceived an ambitious dream which gradually took shape through his persistence.

Various elevation drawings produced around 1842 reveal that major decisions had already been taken in terms of architectural approach. And they show that, between what was planned in the design – which we believe to be the work of von Eschwege – and what was eventually built, there were very few structural alterations. So, between 1840 and 1842, the renovation of the monastery and its improvement continued, with the erection of the clock tower, an interesting and early pastiche of the Torre de Belém. From 1842 to 1843 the forecourt of the chapel was extended and the boundary walls put up, with their Moorish-style arches and the little belvedere shaped like an Arab minaret. The neo-Moorish arches that encircle the structure of the monastery and allow enjoyment of the surrounding views must date from the same time, and it was almost certainly Dom Fernando who designed the fascinating new gateway – with its heraldic and esoteric references – which comes before the older entrance; and it was also the king who added the drawbridge.

41

Prospecto do Palacio novo de a Frente Principal

Above: Prospecto do Palacio novo de a Frente
Principal *(View of the new Palace, main façade),*
unsigned and undated (1842?), Indian ink and grey
watercolour on paper (Pena National Palace collection).
This elevation, solely of the New Palace, shows in greater
detail what was planned and what was actually carried
out. It confirms the elimination of the chimneys and the
disappearance of the bay window from the central
structure that links with the great cylindrical tower.
On the other hand, the bow-window of the main structure
is retained, serving the noble floor and what was to
become the Indian Room. Beneath this window the
inflected door, built from a simple design by Eschwege,
was substituted by the famous Triton or "monster" Portico.
The central structure was simplified when the work
was carried out, with just one projection instead of four,
as far as we know inspired by the pattern on the façade
of the palace at Mafra. Similarly, the windows of the floor
of the Noble Room, which are shown on the drawing with
a neo-Manueline design, were replaced by simpler windows
of an unusual design (the perfect-curve embrasures are
surmounted by circular oculi). The cylindrical tower,
in the construction phase, was surmounted by a large
semi-spherical cupola, whilst the towers of the side
structure were each topped by a bulbous cupola

Opposite, above: Plan and cross-sections of the
initial design of the New Palace, to be added to the
Manueline structure of the monastery
(Pena National Palace collection)

Opposite, below: Projecto do Terraço Norte
ou Pátio dos Arcos, da Torre do Galo e dos
Aposentos da Rainha (Design of the North Terrace
or Pátio dos Arcos, the Torre do Galo and the
Queen's Chambers), Indian ink and grey water-
colour on paper, unsigned and undated (1842?)
(Pena National Palace collection). This has the
peculiarity of showing the large circular tower
before the change it underwent, as well as the
structure of the New Palace, in cross-section.
Alongside this can be seen the continuation of the
arched vaults surmounted by the Torre do Galo,
which was to be changed, and below this the
elevation of the neo-Moorish arches of the terrace

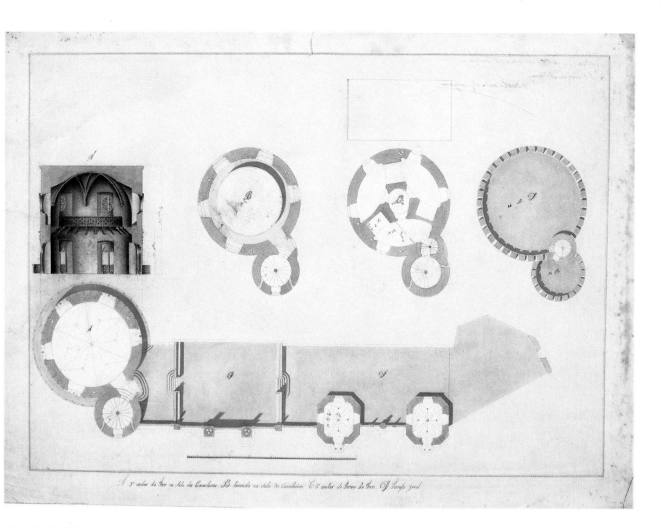

A 3.º andar da Torre ou Sala dos Cavaleiros. B Varanda na chula dos Cavalheiros. C 1.º andar de Torre da Fore. D Perespetiva geral.

A Perspile interior das Aguadaeira inferior de bains pelo do lado principal e das necitas. B Perspile de Pateiral com currectoi es louei na inferior de Pala. C Perspile esterior de Meuno D Perspile em Andas no lado n.º 15.º

Torre do relógio do palácio real da Pena (*Clock tower of the Pena Royal Palace*), *lithograph, drawn and engraved by Legrand, dated 1843* (*Pena National Palace collection*)

Having decided to build the New Palace – the initial plan for this part of the building dates from 24 December 1842 – and now on the basis of the drawings, construction began concurrently on the rectangular structure of the stables, coach-houses, kitchens and servants' accommodation, a building which links with the New Palace, the construction of which had already begun (it would not otherwise have made sense to plan it in that place and in that form). Building continued without interruption until 1846, and the handing of the 'plan of works' to the master mason João Henriques dates from the following year, which suggests a perfect knowledge of what was planned. In 1852 stained glass windows were installed and the restoration of the chapel was completed. In 1853 the foundations were laid for the twisted columns on the exterior of the New Palace. From 1854 the project of decorating the interior of the New Palace

and of the 'little convent' began, in the Sala Árabe and the Quarto da Rainha. When three years had passed, the Sala dos Embaixadores – later the Sala do Bilhar and now the Salão Nobre – was surfaced with plaster. With the participation of the monarch, who kept a close eye on the work, the following years continued to be devoted to decoration, as Ruhl's designs date from this period – although these were not in fact used – as well as the commissioning of various furnishings and fittings (furniture from Dejante, ironwork from Dupire and lamps from Margotteau).

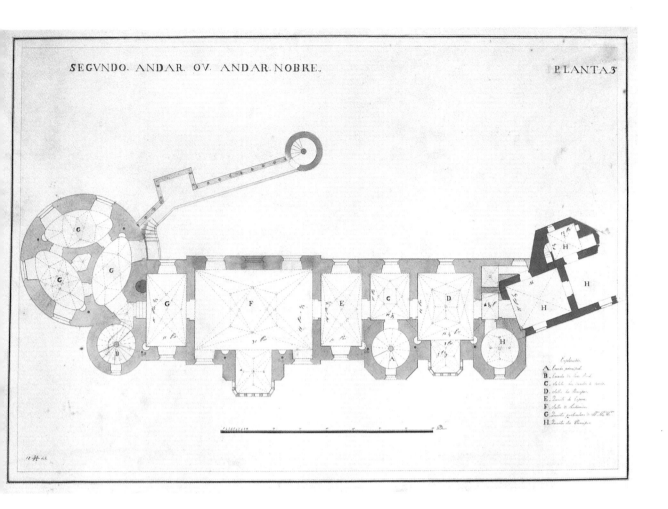

Above: SEGVNDO ANDAR. OV. ANDAR.
NOBRE (*SECOND FLOOR OR NOBLE FLOOR*),
*plan drawn in Indian ink and grey watercolour
on paper, attributed to Nicolau Pires, dated
24 December 1842 (Pena National Palace
collection). If we compare the present plan of the
building with the design, we can see that few
structural changes were made. In this building,
the changes are on the outside and almost all of
them are decorative*

Left: Prospecto do Palacio a Castellado da Pena
do Lado Sul (*View of the Fortified Pena Palace
from the South*), *unsigned and undated (1842?),
Indian ink and grey watercolour on paper
(Pena National Palace collection)*

Work on the Pena Palace is recorded until 1885,
the year of Dom Fernando's death, but the project was
already essentially complete around the middle of the
nineteenth century, when a considerable quantity of
drawings, engravings and watercolours were produced
of the monument in its present form – with a greater
or lesser approximation to reality, with more or less
fantasy – because it had now taken on its final form.

The direct administration of the work and the
influence of the monarch were what determined the

45

Above: Frente do Palácio novo pelo lado
do Este (*Design of new Palace seen from
the East), unsigned, undated (1842?)
(Pena National Palace collection)*

'language' of the building. The revivalist architecture to be found in it seems to constitute a compromise between three stylistic approaches: Germanic neo-Gothic; the contemporary interpretation of the Manueline style; and the introduction of constant oriental elements. These were to symbolize, in short, the exploits of the Portuguese discoveries, through a nineteenth-century Romantic tradition. We are led to believe that the more oriental aspect of the style is due to von Eschwege (taking the form of a quite unusual neo-Moorish and in some features Moghul style, gathered from examples and designs in circulation, of English origin, possibly based on examples such as Sezincote House, in Gloucestershire, completed 1807, or on the 'Ottoman' revivalism in the Royal Pavilion at Brighton, designed by John Nash). Dom Fernando was responsible for the more nationalist neo-Manueline decorative choices. In other words, the baron was responsible for the outline of the whole palace and some options of a more academic nature – if they can be called that – whilst the king was responsible for the specific choices which, nevertheless, reveal the eclectic and purely 'Portuguese' (or Sintraesque) image of the whole, as we will see, as we take a look around the exterior of the palace.

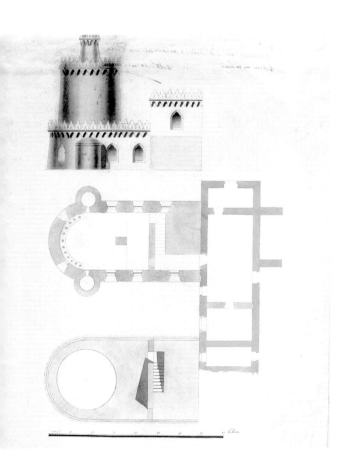

Left: Plan of the circular tower, which is shown joined onto the main wall to the west, unsigned and undated, pencil drawing with grey and pink watercolour (Pena National Palace collection)

Below: Pena Palace in the final phase of construction. Photograph, Tisseron (Ajuda Library collection). Note the scaffolding attached to the façades. This documents the last stage of painting and the installation of tiles

The Exterior

ENTRANCE GATEWAY

Entry to the grounds of the Pena Palace is through a monumental gateway inspired by Moorish military architecture, set in a wall surmounted by a row of merlons. The internal division of the lower embrasure of the curve is outlined in a horseshoe shape. The arch is ornamented by simulated ashlar, used also in the rectangular moulding, and topped by a simple keystone. It stands on two columns with smooth shafts, with capitals decorated with an Egyptian-style wave motif, with the same thing happening at the bases, which consist of three rings. The tablet, which is practically cubic, is worked in relief in a pattern of wedges in an Islamic (or Turkish-Ottoman) allusion. The tympanum is covered with decorative tiles, believed to be the work of Cifka. The ornamental details of this piece – certainly one of the last to be integrated into the whole – are distinctive. On the keystone on the side of the vestibule there is an 'open hand' depicted in relief, a motif of hermetic characteristics which seems to refer to the symbolism of royal justice, and at the same time showing the 'royal' status of the residence; and that the enclosure constitutes, presumably as a whole, a place gifted with magical properties. The hand thus functions as a talisman against the evil eye (Regina Anacleto). On the outside, the tympanum has three open roses arranged in a triangle; and on the inside, one rose in flower. Among many others, these motifs have been interpreted as symbolic of the Rosicrucian affiliation of Dom Fernando II. A more prosaic interpretation connects them with family heraldry, since the royal arms include the form of a rose.

General view of the New Palace and of the building of the former Monastery. Below, the buttresses of the access tunnel

Gateway decorated with tiles and a symbolic rose

THE COACH HOUSE

Facing the visitor is the coach house, with a façade of two storeys on the side of the atrium and another of four storeys towards the slope of the Serra. The frontispiece has a symmetrical composition, with a horseshoe-shaped arched doorway in the centre, surmounted by a neo-Manueline double window. The other embrasures are of two types: one a perfect curved arch surmounted by an awning in squared stone, on the upper floor; the other of neo-Moorish design, at ground-floor level.

Jutting out to the left of this structure is the cylindrical bulk of the watchtower, which provides a magnificent viewpoint over the park. It is crowned by a bulbous Islamic-style cupola, covered in yellow tiles with a blue band close to the base. The corona of the building consists of merlons cut in oriental shapes, delineating the whole terrace. The south façade of this building has projecting balconies, which are a typological compromise between the balconies of the Torre de Belém (see, for example, their support on modillions) and balconies from Indian civilian architecture (in a Moghul style or Goanese model, according to the representations which are to be found in the seventeenth-century album of Jan Huyghens von Linschoten). This well reflects the oriental-style revivalism of the Pena Palace. Behind stands the great cylindrical structure, in line with the scheme of composition established in the initial project.

The upper terrace gives access to a building containing the kitchens, next to it, a formally more modest construction in area and volume, but distinguished by the same type of corona. Inside, the kitchens, as they back on to the large cylindrical tower of the New Palace, link via a semicircular corridor with the enigmatic and original Sala de Jantar (Dining Room), now the Sala dos Veados (Stag Room). The 'chimney' of the kitchens is a small but splendid miniature treatise on medieval revivalism, to a unique design, and is one of the most predominantly vertical elements in the whole structure.

From here, the visitor immediately gets a sense of the monumental nature of the palace and, above all, of the different successive levels of the various constructions, and is able to examine the coherence of the whole building.

Top: View of the first terrace with the coach house building

Bottom: Terrace of the coach house building. Detail of the minaret

Above: View of the former Monastery and Chapel from the tower of the New Palace

Left: Chimney of the royal kitchens. Exterior view

Flower container at the entrance to the access tunnel

THE MONUMENTAL GATEWAY

This is one of the most curious elements in the whole exterior of Pena Palace. It comes before a drawbridge and was added to the original gateway, with its escutcheon, around 1843–44. It is an almost autonomous architectural piece in its design, distinguished from the rest of the façades by the density of the ornamental and decorative details. In compositional terms, it consists of an arch entrance, cut into a wall crowned by five merlons, the largest of which is in the centre. On either side is a watchtower, replicas of the watchtowers of the Torre de Belém, although redesigned. The drawing for the project, unsigned but attributed to Dom Fernando II, shows that this is in response to a specific wish of the monarch, as he had originally designed two types of watchtower and later opted for a different model, which he also drew and accompanied with notation instructing the masons to construct these 'in place of the others'.

The whole structure works towards a thematic synthesis, with an accumulation of ornamental motifs from sixteenth-century buildings in Lisbon, in some way associated with the 'idea' and the conception of the Manueline style, in its nineteenth-century vision. The moulding of the door is decorated with 'balls' (repeated in other parts of the palace), in a clear imitation of the famous Cunhal das Bolas, which still stands in the Bairro Alto in Lisbon. The other decoration, a protruding diamond design, in turn imitates the façade of the famous Casa dos Bicos, a waterside building dating from around 1520. The same theme is repeated in the external ornamentation of the watchtowers. Partially reproducing the watchtowers of the Torre de Belém, as we have seen, each of the watchtowers of the palace is roofed with a characteristic sectioned cupola, a motif interpreted since then as being of Indian origin. They are edged with cornices with a typical Manueline twisted-rope design.

Each impost of the arch has two intertwined serpents sculpted in relief, a rather intriguing motif, but one perfectly consistent with the symbolic and magical conception that guided the construction of the palace. Their significance is hard to decipher exactly, but suggests the concept of unity, considering the extremely long tradition from which the depiction of the serpent comes – a symbol so broad and polysemous that its final purpose is hidden from us. In any case, these serpents are located at the entrance to the palace, side by side with the animals that serve as supports to each watchtower – the head of a lion on the left and that of a reptile or dragon, on the other – as though reinforcing the apotropaic nature of the entrance, serving as guardians of the residence. They join with the helmet depicted in relief on the keystone of the arch, symbolizing the 'chivalrous dignity' of the castle – which is in reality almost a 'temple' to traditional chivalry.

Left: General view of all the entrance porticos. The one on the left is the main entrance to the palace, also known as the Porta Férrea (Iron Gate), which gives access to the 'spiral' tunnel

Right: Monumental gateway or Porta Férrea

Above, the merlons have an even stranger decoration. On the broadest one, in the centre, the chivalrous character of the whole building is reasserted, in the form of two crossed swords (forming an 'x'); on the others, appear crosses of the Order of Christ, of which the monarch was a member, suspended from animal skins. These skins may be the representation of the golden lamb of myth, associated with the Order of the Golden Fleece, which was also bestowed upon Dom Fernando. Analysed more carefully, however, they look more like wolf skins, as though asserting a para-Masonic programme, since the title 'young wolves' was conferred on initiates or neophytes (or on the 'sons' of initiates) in one of the Masonic rites. The motif might also relate to Martinist symbols of initiation.

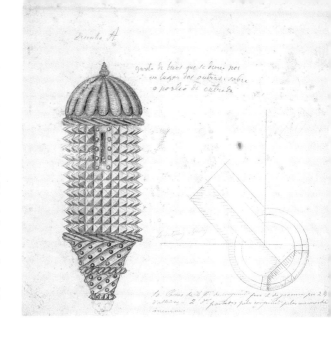

Top: Drawing of the gateway that comes before the drawbridge, probably by Dom Fernando II, pencil on paper. Inscription: "Instead of these watchtowers, the watchtower with points should be used". "Sr. Nicolau/The watchtowers on the corners/should have points/on the corners, as/drawing A attached shows"

Above: Detail of the drawing of the watchtowers that were to fortify the elevation of the Porta Férrea. Inscription: "Drawing A/ Watchtower with points, which should be used/instead of the others, on/the entrance gateway", *unsigned and undated, pencil drawing on paper (Pena National Palace collection)*

Left: General view of the monumental gateway or Porta Férrea, with revivalist and symbolic architectural motifs. This comes before the older monumental gateway and accommodates the drawbridge

The ritual of the Martinist Order, inspired by the writings of Louis-Claude de Saint-Martin (a disciple of Martins Pascoal, who was of Portuguese jewish ancestry), possibly Portuguese and with influences from the Paracletic doctrine of the Three Ages of Joachim of Fiore, included the use of the mask of a 'wolf' for its members.

In other words, the initiatory tone, whether used profoundly and programmatically, or thematically and playfully, throughout the architecture, seems to be expressed in a very clear way at the entrance to the palace. It is known that Dom Fernando frequented Masonic circles (although he was not a member of the Lisbon lodges), following in the footsteps of his ancestors and relatives, who were also involved in various movements of a Masonic or para-Masonic nature, such as the order of chivalry Zur Blauen Erde, of which the monarch's uncle, Prince Leopold of Saxe-Coburg, was a member.

Immediately after this is the original gateway, constructed around 1841, consisting of a hexagonal tower in the centre, flanked by two circular turrets. It is therefore contemporary with the belt of walls and circular buttresses crowned with merlons, which support and encircle the lower level of the building. In the central panel of the main tower can be seen the coat of arms of Dom Fernando. Through this 'fortified' gateway, from which a drawbridge was lowered, we enter the tunnel that leads to the first terrace. These elements establish the hermetic character of the castle

Above, left: Detail of the monumental gateway or Porta Férrea. *Corbel with representation of an animal (a wolf?) supporting one of the watchtowers*

Above, right: Detail of the monumental gateway or Porta Férrea. *Battlements with the heraldic representation of wolfskins (?) and hanging with the Cross of the Order of Christ in relief*

Right, below: Detail of the monumental gateway or Porta-Férrea. *Impost with the representation of snakes*

and form a unit which is similar to an 'antechamber', the purpose of which seems to be 'to prepare the visitor or perhaps the initiate' (Regina Anacleto) who is entering this intricate and enigmatic palace.

THE TERRACE

On the terrace we get our first complete view of the monument. To our right stands the mass of the original monastery, painted in old rose. To the left, covered in tiles of a predominantly blue pattern, stands the New Palace. This group then extends into the large circular tower and the other buildings that are connected to it, all painted in 'Austrian' yellow. The colours correspond to the initial plan from the time of Dom Fernando and were restored after research carried out by the Instituto Português do Património Arquitectónico. The pre-existing elements therefore stand out clearly from those which were added.

Note carefully the true outer wall formed by the two-storey arcades that encircle the old monastery. This winding structure is surmounted by a curious balustrade, decorated with themes inspired by the railings of the balconies of the Torre de Belém – moulded Crosses of Christ – once more referring to imagery expressive of the overseas discoveries, and to their celebration.

Left: Round tower.
General view

Right: Exterior view

THE TRITON PORTICO

In the structure of the new palace itself the so-called Triton Portico is of particular importance and interest. It is also referred to as 'an allegory of the creation of the world'. The embrasure has a lintel with an inflected curve, with four archivolts in conventional neo-Gothic style. It is, however, surrounded by profuse vegetation and by coral forms that almost obscure it, revealing the maritime interpretation of the Manueline style, current at the time and the inspiration for this composition.

In fact the bow-window is supported by a kind of gigantic corbel. On this, seated on a giant clam shell, is the sculpture of a 'monster' – a chimera, half-man, half-fish, with a terrible expression – like a representation of the hideous Adamastor created by Camões in his Lusíads. The hair takes the form of tree-trunks and vegetation, which then forms the stems of a grapevine that encircles the whole window. This is a kind of giant, supporting the weight of the building. It is believed that the inspiration for this sculpture and the elements that surround it may have been taken from the equally extraordinary bust which supports the window of the Manueline sacristy at the Convento de Cristo in Tomar (dated 1510–13). This was for a long time thought to be a celebration of the discoveries; the plant motifs evident within it – dry tree-trunks – were erroneously taken to be corals, in allusion to the seafaring exploits of the Portuguese. In the Pena Palace the motif is repeated, but in caricature or in such an exaggerated way that it produces a unique image in European Romanticism. The symbolic

synthesis is remarkable: the mineral, plant and animal elements are brought together to create architecture properly speaking. Water is represented in the shells; earth in the dry trunks supported by the hybrid figure and in the abundant vegetation which bursts from this in a redemptive display – the grapevines; air, in the clam shells on either side of the Triton; fire is presumed to be creation itself.

The entrance over which the magnificent monster rises leads to a passage which is also elaborately decorated, the 'covered vestibule'. Above it is a vaulted panelled ceiling in the form of trumpets. The whole vault and the walls of the passage are decorated with geometric motifs of a neo-Moorish kind, a probable reinterpretation of the designs commissioned from the Spanish artist Juan de Lizasoaín. Although usually made of wood or plaster, they are here transposed into stone, which is a remarkable artistic and technical achievement. A small vestibule follows, opening on to the Pátio dos Arcos, framed by a doorway consisting of two columns with elevated capitals and geometric decoration, supporting an entablature and a densely ornamented arch, certainly inspired by motifs taken from oriental textiles, in a complex cross between the Ottoman and a vaguely Indian-style impressionism. On either side of this tunnel are two aedicules (niches) or vestibules preceded by neo-Moorish arches. They are roofed by a cupola and decorated with tiles designed by Wenceslau Cifka, depicting medieval panoplies, in yet another reference to the theme of chivalry.

In the niche on the left-hand side is the Porta das Cabaças, which serves as access to the Salão Nobre (Noble Hall). The mouldings are ornamented with

Above: The Triton rises up over the arch and serves as a corbel to the bow-window of the Indian Room. The decoration depicts plants combined with sea, earth and fire motifs

Right: Triton Portico representing 'the creation of the World'. General view

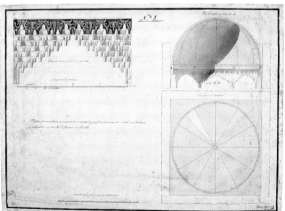

Top: Gallery giving access to the Pátio dos Arcos through the Triton Portico. Detail of the ceiling decoration of Moorish inspiration

Above, left: Dismounted horseman by a creeper of gourds. Engraving by Dom Fernando II

Above, right: Elementary drawing depicting the Moorish decoration of the gallery, signed Juan de Lizasoaín, undated, Indian ink and watercolour on card
(Pena National Palace collection)

Left: Window of the Manueline Sacristy of the Convento de Cristo in Tomar (Diogo de Arruda, 1513)

Left: Another general view of the interior gallery of the Triton Portico

Right; Porta das Cabaças

Below: Detail of the decoration of the Triton Portico gallery

Below left: General view of the gallery. In the centre, the niche framing the Porta das Cabaças

Above: Tiles of the exterior of the gallery of the Triton Portico depicting medieval panoplies

63

Above: Terrace of the Pátio dos Arcos

THE PÁTIO DOS ARCOS

leaves, flowers and gourds in relief, which sprout from two urns. This play between architecture and plant forms is an expression of the neo-Manueline assimilation of the 'original' style of the sixteenth century that served as its inspiration; the Manueline style was based on this symbiosis between structure and ornament. The door itself could have been produced to designs by the king himself. We may be in the presence of yet another manifestation of symbolism, following the traditional interpretation of the gourd as synonymous with plenty, but also as a fortunate recipient, especially when associated with pilgrimage (or with initiation...).

Left: The New Palace building with window and oculus, in the façade inspired by the Manueline sacristy of the Convento de Cristo at Tomar

Coming out of this passageway we enter the Pátio dos Arcos. The structure of the palace proves to us that the Triton was inspired by the famous Manueline window at Tomar. In fact, a curious adaptation of that monument can be seen over the entrance arch. But here it seems to be inverted, since the circular oculus is beneath the window (and not above, as in the original version). As for the window, the design of which was commissioned from Nicolau Pires by the king, this is a 'flatter' and in some ways simplified version. We believe that a good part of the inspiration motivated by the monumental window which Dom Fernando so admired – to the point of ordering the dismantling of the upper structure of the small Renaissance cloister which, at Tomar, partially concealed it – was exhausted when it was translated and reinterpreted in the Pórtico do Tritão. Hence its more modest version in a façade which was, in any case, secondary. The rose or oculus is surrounded by shells and 'mirrors' the spiral decoration at Tomar, although with the rotation reversed. What we have here is an explicit expression of the achievement of the Manueline, understood as a 'national' style in commemoration of the discoveries.

This is due not only to Varnhagen, but also to Edgar Quinet, who disseminated internationally, in a small work published in 1857, the Romantic idea that made this artistic style the expression of the maritime

*Above: General view of the Chapel
from the Pátio dos Arcos*

*Right: Detail of the arch, column
and capital, with Moorish and
neo-Ottoman style decoration*

*Opposite: Detail of the interior of
the gallery leading into the Pátio
dos Arcos*

discoveries. At the end of the nineteenth century, the German scholar Albrecht Haupt finally authorized this view of things in academic circles, since, according to him, it was 'evident that the rapturous splendour of the buildings of India made a deep impression of true fascination on the spirit of the colonizers… and this is why you can clearly see in numerous important buildings certain details imitated not only from India but also from the far east'. It seems obvious that the Pena Palace played the role of a decisive catalyst in the invention – and re-invention – of the Manueline style…

While this is appropriate for later monuments, in the case of Pena Palace it makes more sense to assert that we are in the presence of an 'epi-Manueline' style, even sometimes a 'counter-Manueline' style. By celebrating and crystallizing the more folkloric forms of the Manueline, it exaggerates and caricatures them, showing above all what true Manueline 'is not'. Nevertheless, by working like this, the neo-Manueline lent itself to ideological appropriation and to a systematic subservience, which distorted what it was necessary to distort in order to convey the message of an enterprising and nationalistic progressivism, which then spread to *fin-de-siècle* buildings.

Returning to Pena Palace and the Pátio das Colunas, the outlook on this side of the building is less animated, although the decorative theory of the windows, neo-Manueline in essence, can still be seen. In front of us extends a broad gallery of arches, which looks out over the wide marshes to the north of Sintra. These are neo-Moorish in design, with the spans surmounted and crowned by bevelled merlons. To the

Right: Doorway of twisted columns in the New Palace building supporting the ceremonial balcony

Below: Tiles from the gallery of the twisted column arch, depicting a fight between two dismounted knights

right rises the structure of the chapel, preceded by a porch, topped by a pinnacle covered with chequered tiles, a building which is more the fruit of restoration than architectural redesign. The clock tower dominates this wing with its obvious allusions to the Torre de Belém, an early forecast of what would later become the castles of the Rhine and their scenographic architecture.

To the left stands a narrow and elongated structure which communicates with the New Palace. On a lower level, corresponding to the former stables, is a Manueline door – believed to be original – framed by a neo-Moorish arch of nineteenth-century construction. The final form of the work does not differ from the drawings, in particular the one showing the 'West Side' (together or as a whole, with the clock tower at one end and the cylindrical turret at the other) or the one representing the 'East Side', which corresponds almost completely to the details of the area of the New Palace seen from this side. Only the design of the embrasures was altered, with the stair tower, more slender, backing on to the great cylindrical tower, added to them.

Above: View of the Palace looking down from the Clock Tower

Right: The New Palace and terrace, viewed from the former Monastery

Returning to the main façade through the embrasure that opens to the visitor's left, we go through a new tunnel decorated with neo-Moorish motifs – multi-lobed blind arches cut into the walls – and with an arch with an entablature paying tribute to the Indian-revival. On the main façade, the archway which gives access to this gallery is flanked by two large twisted columns imitating the Puerta de Justicia of the Alhambra in Granada, a delicate work of stereotomy in stone, once more combining Moorish elements with Manueline additions (like those of the twisted columns of the Mosteiro de Jesus in Setúbal). They support the main veranda of the Salão Nobre.

Once more we can appreciate the ensemble formed by the façade of the New Palace and the linking of the structures, from which the imposing cylindrical tower stands out. Note the disconcerting variety of the embrasures, predominantly neo-Manueline (multi-lobed arches, coiled patterns, half roses) in a whole which is clearly intended as exotic architecture, in an attempt to make the imaginary bridge between West and East, yet using a new composition of stylistic vocabularies, neo-Gothic and Islamic forms, and diffuse syntheses of Indian orientalism and Germanic decorativism, leading to a disconcerting syntax and the creation of a new language.

Left: Patterned tiles in the New Palace

Right: Patterned tiles

The Interiors

An inspection of the interior of the Palace has to be made via the usual route for visitors. A proportion of the rooms have undergone full or partial restoration. Having been subjected to various forms of occupation and arrangement, they are now small repositories of memory. So the aim has been to reconstitute, on the basis of the descriptive, narrative and graphic documentation, their original layout and ambience and to fill them with furniture, as far as possible original, in order to achieve this end.

Passing from one room to another, however, we follow not only the route of the ordinary visitor, but also a rational arrangement of spaces; so that the surprise gradually generated by the different spaces, in spite of their predominantly small scale, can be felt. It is to be believed that, without prejudice to the spatial constraints to which the palace was subject because of its attachment to the former monastery, the programme of ornamentation decided on by Dom Fernando took consideration of all these aspects, retaining a sense of occlusion, mystery and shelter, in stark contrast – a Romantic one, besides – to the harshness of the climate at the top of this magical mountain range.

Bearing in mind the uses of the palace's rooms, the aim has also been to show to the public as faithfully as possible the spirit of the rooms as they were inhabited, keeping in view the taste of the *fin-de-siècle* period. The familiarity of the rooms lived in and occupied by the royal personages, the furniture that they chose for their many day-to-day uses, the favourite objects that they touched, the places and the intimacy of the rooms where they most liked to sit and read or take tea, are treated in such a way as to recreate this lifestyle of the end of the nineteenth century.

The intimacy of the rooms is conveyed through the details of daily life, in the taste for reading and in the constant exchange of a great deal of correspondence, the details of a slower way of life, in which the drama of the sentiments, of deep fears and of the transience of happiness was played out on the opera stage. The psychology of this time, understood through rituals of clearly defined etiquette for each hour of the day, led to the fulfilment of nature in a more studied and patient manner. Mourning was more drawn out, since time was not thought of moment by moment but lived slowly. The taste for tobacco, for reading (out loud when in company), for needlework for the ladies, for cricket, tennis, billiards and walking in the open air, these were activities undisturbed by the ticking of the clock. This is how a cultured and elegant society lived, where the subtlety of sentiments was concealed in the well starched folds of a handkerchief, in the small dried leaf pressed between the pages of a book or, even, in the slow telling of prayers with the rosary beads. The multiple reflections of daylight and candle-light, or of lamplight, allowed the piano keys – the musical instrument of Romanticism *par excellence* – to exhale barcaroles or berceuses, like sighs from the soul. Refractions of Time.

THE CLOISTER

Entry to this set of buildings is through an antechamber decorated by the Royal Flag of Dom Pedro V, maintained there since 1861, to mark the death of his son. In this quadrangular-shaped interstitial space there are two U-shaped flights of stairs, which give access to the

Sala dos Veados (Stag Room)

cloister of the former monastery, to overcome the difference in level between the small entrance courtyard, with its oriental references, and the monks' enclosure.

At the base of the stairs, a pair of neo-Manueline columns gives the visit its theme. They are isolated, with the base of the shaft marked by three coiled bands, ornamented with billets which continue upwards to form the handrail. The rest of the surface is decorated with spirals. Each column is crowned by a pseudo-capital at the top, decorated with flowers and grotesque faces in the Manueline style. In this peculiar position, with no structural function other than to indicate the base of the stairs, these columns seem to be designed to mark the symbolism of the palace or some para-Masonic purpose, in such a way that the shape of these two architectural elements is reminiscent of the twin columns of the Temple of Solomon, shown in so many engravings documenting the attributes and symbols of freemasonry.

Once through a neo-Manueline doorway with a three-lobed lintel, we come at last to the monks' cloister.

General view of the cloister

Substantially restored, it retains the look of the original building. There are two storeys, with the elevation divided by a cornice in the form of a rope, which runs across all four façades. Both the lower and upper galleries are vaulted. In the middle of each side, a powerful Manueline-style buttress supports the structure of what was the actual heart of the old Jeronymite Monastery. On the lower floor, each side has two pairs of perfect curve arches. On the upper floor, the galleries open out via six segmented arches. Both the arches of the upper floor and those of the lower floor are supported by columns of characteristic sixteenth-century design, with a multi-faceted base, bevelled shafts and 'mass-produced' capitals carved from local grey limestone. The buttresses and the corners of the cloister are surmounted by Manueline pinnacles with

Cloister, with a view of the central fountain

torsade ornament, similar to that which tops the church of the convent of Nossa Senhora da Conceição at Beja.

This group of buildings is an embellished version of a sixteenth-century cloister, since it is supposed that the vaulting of the upper galleries is original, when they were generally covered in timber framing. This reveals that the original project, determined by Dom Manuel I, was in fact a prestigious one, reflecting the esteem in which that king held the Jeronymite friars, in spite of the small scale of the undertaking. The considerable and careful work of vaulting the chapel, the refectory and other rooms, as well as the subsequent furnishing of the monastery and the other decorative elements, which were gradually introduced during subsequent reigns, are evidence of its relative impor-

tance in the hierarchy of Portuguese religious houses.

The surfaces of the walls are entirely covered, on the outside, with Hispano-Arabic sixteenth-century cord tiles. In a Renaissance or Moorish design, most are from a recorded order placed in Seville for 12,000 tiles, received in 1512. Parts have been restored and it is likely that the missing tiles were ordered to be applied by Dom Fernando, from the state stores set up by the Marquis of Pombal after the famous Lisbon earthquake in 1755, possibly coming from unconnected buildings.

In the centre of the cloister stands the flower vase, a work of the Romantic campaign, composed of a large shell supported by four turtles.

Around the cloister are ranged the cells of the monks and the rooms of more important utilities, which Dom Fernando ordered to be remodelled in their entirety in order to return them to their former reception functions, but with the necessary and required comfort for use by the royal family.

THE PRIVATE DINING ROOM

The entrance to the private Dining Room is through the present scullery, duly furnished with a Portuguese-made dresser with a display of various valuable items, including the Limoges-Haviland service ordered by the Portuguese royal family. This was a regular meeting place in the pattern of palace life for the members of the royal family, whenever they were in residence.

The Dining Room has retained its Manueline architectural structure, with a double spanned vault of starred ribs. Only the surfaces of the walls and the planes of the vault were subjected to intervention and were decorated in patterned tiles,

commissioned in Lisbon from the German manufacturer Eugénio Roseira (Rosenbaum) and applied around 1867. The Dining Room is now arranged to recreate the atmosphere of Dom Fernando's time and set to receive twelve dinner guests. It is furnished and equipped accordingly, with cupboards, sideboards, a Turkish carpet, door-hangings and curtains of Swiss lace at the window. The centre of the table has the most distinctive decorative piece: a stylized caravel held up by figures of Neptune and nymphs, standing on a base with feet representing tritons. A gift from the 'ladies of Paris' to Dona Amélia de Orléans on the occasion of her marriage to Dom Carlos de

Above: Scullery

Left: One of the German silver salvers

Right: Private Dining Room

78

Bragança, future King of Portugal, on 22 May 1886, it is the work of the French goldsmiths Froment Maurice and Louis Aucoc, and it was left to the Pena Palace in the queen's will.

THE CHAMBERS OF DOM CARLOS I

The next rooms correspond to the bedroom, work-room and utility rooms used by Dom Carlos I during his periods of residence. The bedroom is furnished with Imperial-style furniture, the bed has a tester and is decorated with cloths from Lyons, a head-board, *chaise-longue* and mirror. Further on are the bath-rooms, one of a more functional nature, the other with the original furnishings (note the toilet lined in wood). The hot and cold shower, from England, was the first of its kind imported into Portugal.

The workroom, both an office and studio, was care-fully chosen to make use of the light from the win-dows. In addition to the painter's implements (paint-box and brushes), a set of seven unfinished canvases

Above: Dom Carlos I, *Portrait by Escolá, end of the nineteenth century (Mafra National Palace collection)*

Below: Chambers of Dom Carlos I. *Painting studio*

Right: Chambers of Dom Carlos I. *Shower and massage room*

Following pages: Chambers of Dom Carlos I. View of the bedroom

on amorous themes ('erotic paintings') are exhibited, to demonstrate the artistic activity of the monarch, practised to the extent that he is considered among the more interesting Portuguese painters of late naturalism. The largest canvas, occupying the entire right-hand wall, depicts the Serra de Sintra with the Pena Palace at the top. In all of these rooms, the structures supporting the lower floor of the little monastery were retained without significant alterations, particularly the vaulted ceilings of the workroom – believed to be seventeenth century – as well as the Manueline arches of the bedroom, without visible corbels, certainly set into the reinforcing walls of the former monastery. Note the magnificent collection of glasses and beer tankards, some of which date back to the seventeenth century.

Above: Chambers of Dom Carlos I. Another view of the studio

Right: Ninfa correndo em Campo de Girassóis *(Nymph running in a field of sunflowers). Painting from a series from the studio of Dom Carlos I. Oil on fabric, nineteenth century, 1893*

THE MONK'S CELL
AND SÃO JERÓNIMO CHAPEL

In the planned restoration, Dom Fernando opted to keep one of the Jeronymite monk's cells intact, and this is recreated here with the austerity that characterized it originally.

In the well of the stairs leading to the second floor of the cloister is a small chapel, built into the space left naturally by the rock. The inlaid decorative work – pieces of porcelain and mother-of-pearl – appears to date back to the seventeenth century. An image of St. Jerome the Hermit presides over this devotional space.

THE CHAPEL

The Chapel of Nossa Senhora da Pena can be reached via a flight of stairs from the cloister, but also from the outside via the Queen's Terrace. It is located obliquely in relation to the rooms of the monastery, demonstrating that it was built earlier than the monastery which Dom Manuel I built. Positioned at the top of the Serra, the monastery was founded in an area where the terrain was easier to work, in spite of the great effort involved in preparing the foundation platform, which was still complex and demanding. On the other hand and for obvious reasons, the Manueline chapel was established on the same site as the earlier one.

On the outside, it was a modest construction, with a plain western façade and a triangular gable-end surmounted by bevelled merlons in a Manueline-Moorish style, which are still in place. As it was necessary to extend the internal space without sacrificing the orientation of the chancel, an interesting linking system was devised. The Manueline modernization added to the existing chancel and nave, defined along the traditional east-west orientation, an extension of equivalent size on a north-south axis, which would become the sacristy and choir. So the Manueline chapel forms an L-shape, solving an architectural problem in an interesting way, and combining liturgical necessities with a link to the new monastery. For this reason, the structure of the church and its additions still appear unusual to us today.

So, if we enter the Chapel by the door which opens on to the outside of the terrace (the secular entrance), the reading of the space is conventional, developing in a normal way, according to the nave/chancel layout. If we enter from the monastery/palace side, through the entrance provided in the cloister for the monks to use – which is now the usual entrance for visitors – a view of the choir/sacristy is obtained, with the end of the church (the chancel) emerging to our right, almost imperceptibly.

This group of buildings must date from around 1507, when, as we have seen, the presence of the mason Diogo Boytac is recorded in Sintra. He was the most distinguished master builder of the Manueline period, confirming the importance given to this task by its patron. The design of the nave, choir and sacristy are probably his, as well as the original chancel, although this underwent later alterations in the reign of Dom João III, in order to receive the magnificent retable which gives it the finishing touch. The system of vaulting, with central keystones without links between them, and ribs forming trapeziums, with the vertices marked by points from where the ribs depart which are set in the corbels of the walls, is an efficient but elegant solution common to other works by Boytac – repeated in the other Manueline rooms of the little convent. The chancel arch is composed of an external moulding with sculptured plant motifs and an interior jamb and arch of great sculptural volume. The walls of the nave are lined with green and white tiles.

It is separated from the sacristy by a screen or balustrade in ebony, on which is a finely designed ark-shaped chest and a shelf with six candlesticks and a crucifix. The walls are also decorated with tiles dating from 1622.

Particularly noteworthy is the stained glass, which was commissioned in 1841, following the instructions of Dom Fernando who ordered 'stained glass in its windows, to impart the mysterious light peculiar to Gothic Churches'. A second commission was made in 1852, also from Germany, and the glass was installed in the windows of the most important rooms of the building. The central window of the nave was produced in Nuremberg (signed *Kerner in Nurnberg, 1841*), but almost certainly designed in Portugal, given the subject matter and its details. The picture was perhaps by King Fernando himself or by the young painter Visconde de Meneses.

At the sides of the window are the Portuguese royal coat of arms and that of Saxe-Coburg-Gotha; in the centre is the armillary sphere and the cross of Christ. To the left, a figure of the Virgin appears to refer to Our Lady of Pena, accompanied to the right by what is presumed to be St. George; below to the right we have Vasco da Gama, with his coat of arms, with a caravel and the Torre de Belém in the background; to the right, King Manuel I exhibits a model of the Pena monastery. The idea was, in short, to include in this picture all the themes of the founding of the monastery, from the miraculous appearance of the Virgin, to the discoveries (Vasco da Gama) and Dom Manuel I, who was the founder, but also the astonished witness in this very place to the return of the fleet of the Portuguese captain in 1502.

Stained-glass window of the Chapel, representing Our Lady of the Pena with the Infant Jesus, St. George, Dom Manuel and Vasco da Gama, made in Nuremberg, Germany, dated 1841

THE RETABLE

The retable of the Pena chapel is one of the master-pieces of the Portuguese and Iberian Renaissance. Presented by Dom João III and Dona Leonor, it was made by the French sculptor Nicolau Chanterene between 1528 and 1532. Chanterene was in Sintra during this period, having spent some time in Lisbon and Coimbra, where he left other fine examples of his work. The retable has an unusual presence, bearing in mind its almost incorporeal nature, achieved by various means, such as simulated architecture, perspectives in depth or in relief, and the union of 'disconnected' or allusive elements, such as the garland which frames the entire piece. Note that another decisive role is given to the use of materials – two types of alabaster, white and black (or blue). The white is used for almost the entire object – backgrounds and figures, garland – whilst the dark alabaster marks out the cornices and columns, providing a skilful indication of the horizontal (cornices) and vertical planes (columns). The movement of this piece is unsurpassable. Note the succes-sive register of different depths, the composition of the elaborate sculptural groups and the function – exploited to the full – of the chiaroscuro, in which the final positioning of the item must not have been accidental.

Overall it is a fine aedicule of classical architecture, within which is formed a kind of grandiose façade two storeys high, interrupted in the centre to make room for two smaller aedicular spaces: one at the top, in the corona; the other, at the bottom, immediately above the place for the Blessed Sacrament. The subjects are drawn from the New Testament and refer to the child-hood of Jesus. Independently of the Christ-centred approach apparent in the whole, they almost all refer also to the Life of the Virgin, in a clear reference to the patron saint of the monastery.

At the top, in the upper aedicule, is the Nativity. Immediately below is the Virgin teaching the infant Jesus to read (a subject certainly promoted by the

Below left: The Chapel retable, detail:
'the Flight into Egypt'

Below right: The Chapel retable, detail:
'the Presentation of the Infant in the Temple'

Right: The Chapel retable by Nicolau Chanterene, c. 1528–32

Jeronymite friars, who were well known for the reading and interpretation of the Holy Scriptures). In the upper sections we have, on the left, the Virgin come upon unexpectedly in her chamber by the Angel Gabriel, whilst a person, coming on an errand, carries a jar on their head (note the movement in the drapery of the dossal); on the right is the Adoration of the Magi. In the lower sections we have, on the left, the Presentation of Jesus in the Temple and, on the right, the Flight into Egypt. At the bottom, the central niche shows the death of Christ. The section in bas-relief of the lower part – at the base – continues with the theme of the life of Jesus, notably the Last Supper, inspired by an engraving by Marcantonio Raimondi. The entire

Quarto das Damas

piece is a testament to the learning of its creator, both in art and the Scriptures. Many of the elements depicted there date from as early as the final years of the 1520s, reflecting the esteem in which the Roman style was then held, as an essential part of the ideological and pastoral modernization of the Church and, in particular, of the Jeronymite friars, whose role was then a reformist one.

In conception, this piece is close to the staging of the 'mysteries' (Dagoberto Markl), since it shows the *mise en scène* of various passages of the Scriptures. The extremely elaborate backgrounds are the key to understanding this complex history.

Nicolau Chanterene played an important role in the development of Portuguese sculpture, in both theme and vocabulary, and his relationship with other contemporary artists and architects seems to have led to the penetration of the syntax of the Renaissance into Portugal. More than a mere retable plain and simple (or solely 'utilitarian', for liturgical purposes), this piece is an important testimony to – practically a small experimental treatise on – classicist architecture. In fact, Chanterene seems to have specialized in the miniaturization of architecture. As represented in the backgrounds of the Pena retable, it attains the level of actual maquettes or models, not to mention the 'monumental' language of the retable itself, intricately perfect in its formulation. Note that the position chosen for its location makes a strong aesthetic statement, opposing the played-out Manueline formulary of the architecture of the chapel, against the vigorous, dense and rhetorical Renaissance arsenal of the sculpture which, here, is also architecture...

THE FIRST TWO ROOMS

Once on the upper floor, after ascending the circular stairway (which also gives access to the turret), we return to the range of former cells, now completely refurbished to incorporate a series of rooms, annexes and offices for the royal family, initially intended for Dom Fernando II and Dona Maria II, but occupied especially by Queen Amélia when she became a regular resident at Pena Palace. The first two rooms – the Quarto do Veador and the Quarto das Damas – are mostly filled with sets of nineteenth-century Portuguese furniture, Romantic in style, with the exception of the bed in the first room which is an Indo-Portuguese eighteenth-century piece. Both rooms have plaster decorations, the first with plant themes – trunks, leaves and pine-cones – the second with floral themes in wreaths, produced by the team of Master Domingos Meira of Afife.

THE QUARTO DA RAINHA (QUEEN'S CHAMBER)

The decorative work done in the Queen's Chamber can be attributed to the painter and designer António Januário Correia, who began work at Pena Palace in August 1854. This includes detailed plaster work, reproducing Moorish tracery patterns over all the surfaces of the walls and ceiling. The dominant tonality is warm and luminous, due to the extensive use of gold-leaf appliqué. It demonstrates the oriental flavour which was created in many of the interiors, in harmony of course with the architectural choices adopted for the exterior of the palace and with the neo-Moorish characteristic of the revivalist aesthetic of the second half of the nineteenth century.

The two keystones of the vaults present, respectively, the royal coats of arms of Dona Maria II and Dom Fernando, and those of Dona Amélia and

Left: Quarto do Veador

Top: Quarto da Rainha (Queen's Chamber)

*Above: Chamber pot with lid,
Companhia das Índias, eighteenth century
(Pena National Palace collection)*

93

Left: The Queen's toilette

Right: Quarto da Rainha (Queen's Chamber)

Dom Carlos I. The furniture, which is eclectic, includes a bed with an eighteenth-century ebony head-board, a neo-Gothic couch, and a sideboard and a bureau also in ebony. The fireplace surround is in walnut, with a decorated fire-guard with embroidery depicting an elegant landscape in the style of Boucher.

Standing out amongst the items exhibited, opposite the mirror with a frame in French silver, is one of Dom Fernando's favourite pieces, which comes in fact from his personal collection: a basin and jug, made in Portugal, from the mid-eighteenth century.

THE QUARTO DE VESTIR
(DRESSING ROOM)

THE SALA DE SAXE
(SAXONY ROOM)

The adjacent Dressing Room is still lined with the original fabric, conferring an intimacy on this small room, containing furniture and accessories – particularly the lamps, commissioned from the house of Gagehaut, Paris – which recreate its function. The dressing-table, a decorative item characteristic of such rooms in the last century, is equipped with silver and crystal toilet articles.

This room is totally decorated with porcelain fittings from Saxony. Entirely nineteenth-century in style, this set of furniture is composed of a bureau, a desk, a sideboard, a pair of candlesticks, a mirror and a central table. The countless ceramic plates are made by various craftsmen from that famous porcelain factory, depicting country scenes, their decoration completed with plant forms.

Above: The Queen's dressing room

Left: Sala de Saxe (Saxony Room)

Below, left: Glass beer tankards from Bohemia, 1683

Below, right: Chest (Ventó) with the arms of Saxony inlaid in the door, nineteenth century (Pena National Palace collection)

THE SALA DE ESTAR PRIVADA (PRIVATE SITTING ROOM) OF THE ROYAL FAMILY

The private sitting room of the royal family – also known as the Gabinete da Rainha or Sala do Espelho – lined in silk damask, provides a fine setting for the Meissen porcelain candle-holders, and for all the pieces which decorate this room.

Once more, the furniture (bookcases, escritoires, sofas, armchairs) is eclectic and varied in provenance. Notable are the marble and bronze sculpture *Nature Revealing Itself through Science*, by E. Barrias, presented to Dom Carlos I on 24 November 1905, on a visit to Paris (giving us further evidence of the monarch's occupation as a distinguished naturalist); and the upright piano with a frame of jacaranda wood. It was in this room that King Edward VII and Queen Alexandra of Great Britain were received in 1903. Notable among the pictures is an oil composition, *Charity,* by the painter Columbano.

Above: Private Sitting Room

Left: Private Sitting Room. Sculpture from the collection of Dom Carlos: A Natureza descobrindo-se perante a Ciência (*Nature Revealing Itself through Science*), *by E. Barrias, marble and bronze, 1905*

Right: Sala de Estar Privada (Private Sitting Room of the Royal Family)

THE ESCRITÓRIO DA RAINHA
(QUEEN'S STUDY)

The next room is the Queen's Study, equipped with a Romantic secretaire and chair, displaying a Meissen porcelain bust of a girl and other personal items. An oil painting on canvas by Cristino da Silva, entitled *Serra de Sintra*, can be seen in this small room. This is an interesting piece which depicts in a contrasting fashion – in the play of shadows, light and celestial background – the romantic atmosphere of Sintra: in the foreground, a young shepherd child watches over his little goats, leaning against one of the crags of the Serra (reminiscent of the drawing done by Dom Fernando in 1839...); on the right, the outline of the Castelo dos Mouros is almost obscured by clouds; in the background, watching over this bucolic scene, is the restored Pena Palace.

Top: The Queen's Study. The intimate atmosphere is recreated by the proliferation of small objects and by the comfortable furnishings

Above: Bust of girl, in Meissen porcelain, nineteenth century (Pena National Palace collection)

Above: Menina (Girl) in porcelain from Saxony. Queen's Study

THE SALA ÁRABE (ARAB ROOM)

This small room – previously known as the Sala do Álbum, as it was here that the palace's book of honour was signed – had its walls entirely refurbished, painted in fresco and tempera by the Italian Paolo Pizzi. This artist, who was to become famous for works in Lisbon and Oporto, was called to Pena Palace in the beginning of autumn 1854. Over a period of six months, he and his artisans – the Frenchman Pierre Bordes and the Spaniard Paulino – executed what is recognized as the most significant *trompe-l'oeil* painting in the palace.

The model drawings, approved by Dom Fernando, were slightly altered during execution, the 'views' that should have appeared in the embrasures becoming architectural motifs, or broad rooms of columns. The work of illusion emphasized the existing architectural elements (walls, corbels, ribs, ceilings), inserting within them false reliefs painted with plant themes and adding false pilasters. Next to the doors, an ornamental

Top: Sala Árabe (Arab Room). General view

Above: Detail of the mural in the Arab Room. Depiction of Pena Palace on the fan-light of one of the windows. The Palace already appears in a form close to its final construction, revealing the building in progress or, at least, an overall knowledge of the project at the time this room was being decorated, by the Italian artist Paolo Pizzi, c. 1854–55

Sala Árabe (Arab Room). General view

motif was created of tree-trunks interwoven with vine leaves and bunches of grapes; on the ceilings are reproduced friezes characteristic of Late Gothic architecture, evoking the 'naturalistic' and sylvan philosophy of the origin of the Gothic, propounded by James Hall at the end of the eighteenth century.

The design gave expression to a traditionalist interpretation, according to which Gothic architecture was derived from the architecture of the 'primitive hut'. Another interpretation consisted of confusing the origin of the Gothic with the early forms of Islamic architecture. And it is along these lines that the room reproduces, as an illusion, extended arches, in the shape of a horseshoe, multi-lobed and pointed, opening into virtual rooms, filled with columns, similar to Arab mosques. This device confers unexpected depth on a room which is actually quite small. From a technical point of view, note the rigour of the artists, who, using *grisaille*, vividly accentuate the chiaroscuro, creating relief and an effective sense of spatial illusion in their subjects, as in the royal arms of Dom Fernando and Portugal, inscribed over one of the main doors. The combination and thematic superimposition that we find here gives substance to the neo-Moorish, neo-Gothic and neo-Indian extravaganza which was the guiding principle in the construction of the palace; and continues the themes sculpted in relief on the various doorways and embrasures of the building. It is the culmination, in short, of the visionary exoticism of Dom Fernando, and lacks not a single Moroccan lamp or oriental carpet. The Sala is extravagantly furnished with Portuguese and Indian pieces, with chairs, cushioned armchairs, a neo-Gothic ottoman and tables in teak and *tissó*.

THE SALA VERDE (GREEN ROOM)

Decorated with frescoes and tempera paintings by António Januário Correia – geometric patterns predominantly in green – this room is furnished with a round table, chairs and a sideboard with ornament in *papier-mâché*. It is one of various rooms that were decorated, including most of the rooms which we have passed through above, according to a colour scheme described in the work orders drawn up at the time. The task of decoration was, in some cases, shared with the Italian Pizzi and his assistants.

Above: Sala Verde (Green Room), decorated in fresco and tempera

Right: Chair with papier-mâché decoration in the Green Room

THE TERRAÇO DA RAINHA (QUEEN'S TERRACE)

The next vestibule leads to the Queen's Terrace and to a gallery. The view from the terrace shows the true scale of Dom Fernando's vision. The various planes of the building's architecture create a captivating appearance of variety, in the colours of the façades and the different languages used in its elevations, and the unexpected linking of the volumes of the palace. From here we can also see the Templo das Colunas and, a little further up, on the Monte do Gigante, the statue of a soldier, representing the physical and metaphysical guardian of the castle. This bronze is probably the work of the sculptor Ernesto Rusconi, and dated 1844. Initially intended to be positioned in one of the niches in the Triton gallery, it was moved here to free this passageway but also in response to the demands of myth at Sintra.

Top: Landscape setting of the Pena Palace

Above: Sundial on the Queen's Terrace

Another curious piece can be seen on this terrace: a sundial, given to Dom Fernando by his personal physician, Baron de Kessler. This has the peculiar quality of 'firing' at midday, by means of an ingenious combination of a lens and a small cannon.

104

THE SALAS DE PASSAGEM (GALLERIES)

The start of this corridor marks the passage from the former monastery to the New Palace. In interior decoration, the first room contains a Portuguese sideboard and, above it, a French painting from the Barbizon School. Beside the window are two Dona Maria style commodes, with pieces of faïence by the ceramicist Wenceslau Cifka.

Of Austrian origin and trained as an agronomist, Cifka was in the group of young people who accompanied Dom Fernando II when he first came to the country of his future wife. He was particularly interested in the Renaissance majolica which the monarch found in Portugal and collected over a long period. Taking inspiration from its decoration, Cifka created ceramic pieces of indisputable artistic quality, and presented Dom Fernando with large circular dishes on which the monarch is depicted, and pairs of urns in varied shapes. Note the unusual piece in the shape of a violin, depicting Dona Maria II and her illustrious consort in circular panels.

The second room contains a 'Winter Garden', so much in the taste of the period, with the profusion of vegetation common in the interiors of nineteenth-century residences.

Above: Ceramic carafes by Wenceslau Cifka (Pena National Palace collection)

Left: Ceramic violin by Wenceslau Cifka (Pena National Palace collection)

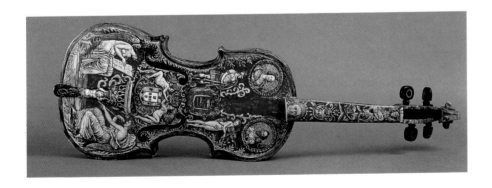

THE SALA INDIANA (INDIAN ROOM)

This room is one of the most interesting from a decorative point of view and one of the most important in the hierarchy of rooms in what is known as the New Palace, opening on to the bow window that is supported on the outside by the huge console of Triton. Its orientation is therefore transverse to the normal lengthways direction of the New Palace. The Indian or oriental allusions are, once more, intentional, if eclectic, reinforced by the teak furniture, all of it of Indian origin – the couch, chairs, centre table, occasional tables and fitted furniture. The marble bas-relief, depicting *Cholera Morbus*, by Vítor Bastos, was purchased by Dom Pedro V, when he visited the sculptor's studio. Also on exhibit are dishes from the Sacavém factory, designed by Dom Fernando II. The partition is covered by a panelled ceiling decorated with neo-Moorish geometric motifs, inspired by designs sent by Juan de Lizasoaín.

Left: Sala Indiana (Indian Room). Corner

Right: Sala Indiana (Indian Room), with detail of the plasterwork, produced under master Domingos Meira, and eclectic ornamentation of oriental inspiration

The plasterwork, attributable to Domingos Meira, is based on Moorish and Indian patterns. These extend over well defined and framed fields, showing their Moorish influence close to the coves – multi-lobed arches in relief, which regulate the transition between the wall panels and the decorated wooden ceiling – and the Indian influence on the other surfaces. Here the abstract geometric nature of acute angles and typically Islamic rectilinear tracery, visible on the ceiling, is replaced by predominantly rounded patterns and a plant theme, possibly taken from tapestry or from sketches or drawings influenced by the remarkable Ottoman and Central European Baroque Revival.

As a small detail, it is worth mentioning that Queen Amélia was particularly fond of using this room for receiving guests at teatime.

Top: Sala Indiana (Indian Room)

Above: Cholera Morbus, *by Vítor Bastos, bas-relief in marble (Pena National Palace collection)*

THE SALA DE RECEPÇÃO (RECEPTION ROOM)

Immediately after this is the Reception Room, a small apartment which is reached by a spiral staircase situated beneath the Triton Portico, through the intriguing ashlar doorway decorated with gourds, the Porta das Cabaças. It was via this room – entirely furnished 'in Indian style' – that guests would enter the communally used rooms of the palace: to the right the more welcoming Sala Indiana and to the left the great Salão Nobre.

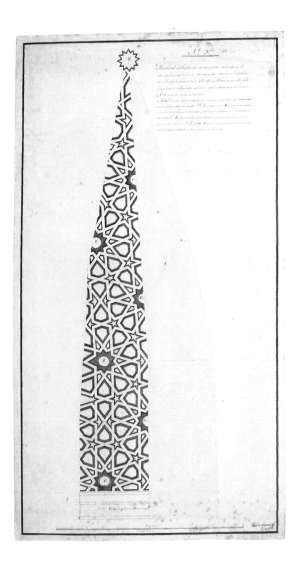

Above: Tea service in cobalt blue
(Pena National Palace collection)

Left: Design used for modelling and creating the decoration of the vault of the Sala Indiana. Drawing no. 3, signed Juan de Lizasoain, undated, Indian ink and blue watercolour on card
(Pena National Palace collection)

THE SALÃO NOBRE (NOBLE HALL)

The reception room *par exellence* and the formal hall for public presentation (and representation), this room, refurbished early on, is decorated with pink and white plasterwork. Making use of the double ceiling height, it presents on its walls various vertical decorative areas of large dimensions, surmounted in a geometrically balanced manner by square panels into which roses are set in relief, as though responding to the rhythm of the external elevations on the south side, with oculi to let in the daylight. This huge task was entrusted to Domingos Meira. His special skill was so appreciated by Dom Fernando II that he conferred on him the Order of Christ.

The furniture is extremely varied, with elements of Indian origin standing out once more, but combined here with characteristically late Romantic furniture.

This is neo-Gothic in reference and it was probably commissioned after the marriage of Dom Fernando to the Countess of Edla in 1869. The exoticism remains, however, emphasized by the imposing presence of four 'candle-holding Turks' sculpted from crabapple wood, each holding a candelabrum for twenty-five candles. They contribute to the lighting of the room, which is otherwise provided by a splendid Late Gothic chandelier with seventy-two candles.

Opposite the main window of the Salão, which looks out over the Triton courtyard, is an oil painting depicting Dom Fernando II as an imposing figure, with the sashes of three Orders (of Christ, Avis and Santiago), and the collar of the Golden Fleece, by Layraud from 1877. Amongst the other paintings is one depicting Dom Fernando dressed as Don Quixote, a carnival scene by Columbano, and the *Passeio Público* (1856), by the Romantic painter Leonel Marques Pereira, one of the Portuguese artists patronized by the monarch. In nineteenth-century Lisbon, the Passeio Público (Public Promenade) – which is no longer there –

1036-B.P.-Cintra-Real Palacio da Pena. (Sala de bilhar.)

Top, left: Candle-holding Turk *(Ambassador's Room)*

Top, right: Chandelier *(Ambassador's Room)*

Left: Salão Nobre *(Noble Room). General view. This is the largest room in the whole palace, a formal reception chamber but also a recreational area for guests, also known as the Ambassadors' Room or Billiard Room*

Above, left: Passeio Público *(Public Promenade), by Leonel Marques Pereira, oil on canvas, 1856 (Pena National Palace collection).*
The 'Artist-King' takes a walk in the company of his secretary, Baron de Kessler and the Conde de Campanhã

Above: 'Salão dos Embaixadores' *(Ambassadors' Room), later the Billiard Room. Postcard, c. 1865 (National Library)*

was a typical Romantic garden. During the second half of the nineteenth century this was to undergo a great boost in social terms, since it was Dom Fernando's favourite place for walking and recreation.

The stained glass in the three windows on the northern side provide echoes of an imaginary chivalry, very much to Dom Fernando's taste, with innumerable heroic and medieval references. These were manufactured in Germany. The present arrangement of the furniture is as it was in the time of Dona Amélia, who was responsible for various acquisitions, and reveals the social pattern that prevailed in this room, orientated towards operatic displays and intimate conviviality.

THE CHAMBERS
OF DOM MANUEL II

The chambers of the last King of Portugal, Dom Manuel II, were situated in the palace's large circular tower. He succeeded his father Dom Carlos I after he was assassinated on 1 February 1908. The first room includes the wooden bas-relief *A Tomada de Arzila*, said

*The Chambers of Dom Manuel II.
First apartment*

*Left: The Chambers of Dom Manuel II.
Bathroom*

*Dom Manuel II. Oil on canvas
portrait by Carlos Reis, 1910
(Pena National Palace collection)*

to date from the sixteenth century and bought at auction in Rome by Dom Fernando. The bedroom is oval in shape, resulting from the division of the upper storey of the tower. The walls were painted a strong red colour – recreating the original wall covering in garnet damask – although the cove, in plasterwork, is still in white, providing a vivid contrast. The furniture, in mahogany, is extremely sober, a combination of Carlos X and Imperial styles. There is also a set of Sèvres porcelain exhibited in a showcase, as well as Romantic furniture and period paintings. The upright piano used by the monarch, who had the celebrated master Viana da Motta as a teacher and is reputed to have been a music-lover, completes the decoration.

Top: Bedroom of Dom Manuel II

Above: The Chambers of Dom Manuel II.
Bathroom. Detail

THE SALA DOS VEADOS (STAG ROOM)

On the lower storey is the Sala dos Veados, a circular room, corresponding to the entire circumference of the great tower of the New Palace, with a cylindrical column in the centre and seven bays. This was unfinished, and the decoration planned for it was never completed. A watercolour by Eugen Ruhl, a German artist responsible for a considerable number of sketches for interior designs, as well as exterior ones for the park area, gives us an idea of the monarch's intentions. This was to display the heraldry of the palace, accompanied by military ensigns showing the royal coat of arms and the Order of Christ, and Dom Fernando's collection of glassware, with a composition of full suits of armour and hunting trophies, consisting of a central column in the form of a tree-trunk, from the top of which sprout leafy branches. The room had been used initially as a dining-room, with, according to its sponsor's instructions, seating capacity for thirty-six guests, a rather curious number which is worthy of note. The change occurred in 1855, when the layout recorded in Ruhl's designs of that year was adopted. It should be noted that it was Dom Fernando's – frustrated – intention, to fill the Park with large game, particularly with deer. Not by chance, certainly, Dom Fernando 'was seen dressed in a garb which would pass for that of a Bavarian hunter' (José Teixeira), since he visited and stayed in the palace frequently.

Without losing in its recreation the function originally reserved for it, the room is now used for temporary exhibitions.

Top: Sala de Armas. *Watercolour on paper by Eugen Ruhl, 1855 (Library of the Ducal Palace of Vila Viçosa)*

Above: Varanda Mourisca (design). *Watercolour on paper by Eugen Ruhl, 1855 (Library of the Ducal Palace of Vila Viçosa)*

Left: Sala dos Veados (design). *Watercolour on paper by Eugen Ruhl, 1855 (Pena National Palace collection)*

Palace kitchens

THE KITCHENS

The kitchens are in a nearby building, in a vaulted area with rounded arches set on quadrangular columns. The remarkable wood stoves, the bread oven, the slow oven and the unusual copper kitchen utensils indicate the importance of ceremony in food preparation in the nineteenth century, with the variety of implements, many of which were bought in Paris in 1863. All of these items are displayed to show the room of gastronomy *par excellence*, and this can be seen in the exceptional collection here. The kitchens open out on to the terrace of the same name.

FROM SMALL MONASTERY
TO LUXURIOUS PALACE

This tour allows us to see the two dimensions of the palace: the adaptations made to the former rooms of the initial nucleus of the monastery, and the more ambitious work carried out beyond its perimeter, expanding into a Romantic project involving a considerable artistic investment. On the other hand, we see the quite fundamental differences in space between the rooms which the old monastery occupies today and the greater expansiveness of those that were designed from scratch. However, the sense of scale is

Top: Aerial view of the Pena National Palace

Above: Covered dish, Ming Dynasty, Qianbing Kingdom, 1736–95 (Pena National Palace collection)

118

not lost between the two. Almost all of them refer to a context of great intimacy, accentuated by the eclectic accumulation of goods, by a certain shortage of space, by the over-accumulation of objects – which was felt necessary in order to incorporate the dimension of luxury and comfort – and by the decorative projects carried out in it, responding to an enrichment which was gradual but consistent with the external architectural expression of the palace.

Above: Queen Amélia in one of the courtyards of the Pena Palace, accompanied by her son, King Manuel II and his favourite dogs (Pena National Palace collection)

Below: The Warrior

PENA PARK

A hundred and fifty years ago it would have been impossible to visualize the luxurious vegetation of the Serra de Sintra and especially, the existence of Pena Park, as almost the entire *serra* was craggy and arid. It is due to Dom Fernando II and to his taste and feeling for nature that, parallel to the construction of the Pena Palace, this magnificent Romantically inspired park was created, extending for nearly two hundred

Above: Pena Park. Arbor vitae

*Right: Pena Park. Tree ferns
by one of the lakes*

hectares of irregular terrain around the great building. The link between the 'constructed' architecture and the architecture of 'nature' corresponds, with unexpected coherence and precocity, to the great project of Romanticism, which had among its aims the urgent reunion with nature – and a reunion with the fortuitousness or 'false fortuitousness' of landscape architecture, to give expression to what Almeida Garrett was celebrating when he wrote: 'Solitude, I salute you! Silence of the woods, hail! I come to you, oh nature; open your heart to me...' (*Flores sem Fruto*, 1845).

It seems certain that the king, when he visited England in 1836, visited the famous Royal Botanical Gardens at Kew, just outside London, and developed a taste which, shortly afterwards, took its form in Pena Park. The park is absolutely inseparable from the palace. The aim was to enhance this surrounding space, through its design (never before seen in Portugal at that time) and through the systematic, dogged and

120

In 1839 the forestation of the *serra* and the organization of the park began, and a task of landscaping followed, continuing practically uninterrupted until the middle of the 1860s, under the constant supervision of the monarch. What is most surprising is the systematic faith in time and in the posterity of things, an essential element in the conception and construction of a park of this kind – but also the working material of Romanticism itself. We do not hesitate to associate Pena Park with a certain air of fraternity, as though it were the intention of the king to restore – or create – his sacred *Urwald*, the primitive forest, to which even the famous giant or Guardian of the Castle would correspond, that species of *Hermanndenkmal*, in other words, a monument to personify the father of the Germanic nation (the Arminius or Hermann of German Romantic tradition, whom Schinkel conceived as a heroic warrior).

Although contributions to the design of Pena Park were many, the design of its plantations and of the numerous garden structures appears to have been by Baron von Eschwege. It is believed that the gardens were laid out with the assistance of Wenceslau Cifka, who, as well as being an artist and amateur photographer, had the necessary professional skill for this, since he had been administrator of the forests of the Reichstadt before settling in Portugal.

Amongst the most significant of the garden buildings is the Templo das Colunas, a small circular hypostyle building, erected around 1840. Inspired by Renaissance open pavilions, it appears as a classicist exercise in its general form and plan, but more eclectic – or Romantic – when looked at in detail. The twelve

persevering planting of a great variety of species. Seed beds and plantations of camellias, tree ferns, chestnut trees, tea plants, Indian chestnuts, walnut trees, ash trees, fig trees, holm oaks, orange trees, pear trees, apple trees, pine trees, cedars, japonicas, arbor vitae, rhododendrons and countless other species, native or imported from Africa, Australia, Brazil, France, England and other countries of northern Europe, are organized in plots duly set out and prepared for each species of tree or bush, in spite of giving the illusion that it has all sprouted and grown there naturally without human intervention. Following the example of Romantic practice, we find ourselves in one of the most significant informal gardens of Europe.

Above: Templo da Colunas

Right: The Countess of Edla's chalet

columns that encircle it are roofed with a bulbous dome, which is in turn divided into a second smaller dome, taking its appearance into the realms of orientalism or stylistic syncretism.

This building, assumed to be Dom Fernando's studio, is more than just a local and well integrated response in the characteristic programmes of informal gardens, being also an important programmatic and symbolic statement. Its location emphasizes one of the two axes established by the exterior of the palace, although it is today practically hidden by the dense vegetation of the park. The decorative themes within it – the cross of Christ – relate the building to the sphere of ideology, to which a large part of Dom Fernando's initiative responded. As though to indicate the recurrent orientalism of all the buildings, the roof is surmounted by a metal crescent. This, in turn, takes on the role of pointing to the 'Mountain of the Moon', evoked by classical writers...

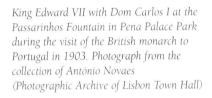

King Edward VII with Dom Carlos I at the Passarinhos Fountain in Pena Palace Park during the visit of the British monarch to Portugal in 1903. Photograph from the collection of António Novaes (Photographic Archive of Lisbon Town Hall)

The Feast of Santa Eufémia promoted by the officials of Pena Palace on 7 August 1900(?), photograph by António Novaes (Photographic Archive of Lisbon Town Hall)

The Passarinhos Fountain was built in 1853 and is one of the many summer houses scattered throughout the park. Almost certainly designed by Baron von Eschwege and built under the supervision of João Henriques, it is one of the keys to understanding the compositional principle of the palace. The structure is heavy, again with oriental references – here Islamic – in its smooth dome. The plan is hexagonal, with twin doors surmounted by a circular oculus, in a somewhat forced reminiscence of a neo-Gothic design, not found elsewhere in the palace. It is entirely covered in pink and blue tiles (supplied by Roseira), and this gives its mocking 'Arabism' a Turkish allusion. The exotic touch continues in the band that ornaments the base of the large dome, where an inscription is written in Arabic characters prepared by von Eschwege and approved by the king: 'The sultan Dom Manuel built this blessed chapel in the name of Nossa Senhora Maria da Pena, in the year 1503, in commemoration of the safe return of Vasco da Gama from the discovery of the lands and countries he found, i.e., the Cape of Good Hope, India and others. Then His Highness the Sultan Dom Fernando Segundo, husband of Her Majesty Dona Maria II built in this way in great royal magnificence, in the year 1840'.

Another curious building is the *cottage orné* or typical English cottage, known as the Casa do Regalo. This is a room intended to be used for picnics and the enjoyment of bucolic evenings, and was built around 1866–67, from masonry, but painted externally in *trompe-l'oeil*, to reproduce beams and planking. The effect is odd and falls within the picturesque approach to garden architecture. This small dwelling became known as the Chalet da Condessa, as the king and his second wife spent their leisure time here in the company of Prince Afonso and mutual friends.

Pena Palace and park constitute an exceptional example, on a European scale, of the affirmation of a culture of landscape. The scenographic dimension of the building conforms to an ordered plan of insertion within its setting. The styles intermingled here reveal a playful lack of distinction that makes this almost a theme park of history and architecture, of an operatic kind. It is not only the epic dimension that has resonance, as we might suppose on a foggy day, clamouring for Mystic Chivalry or the initiatory secrets of a Wagner epic; sometimes, looking at the small scale of its salons, at the intricate, almost embroidered, decoration of many of its elements, you can also hear the harmonies of Rossini or the jesting scenes of Verdi. This is scenography in stone.

BIOGRAPHICAL NOTES

DONA MARIA II (1819–53)

With the full name of Maria da Glória Joana Carlota Leopoldina da Cruz Francisca Xavier de Paula Isidora Micaela Rafaela Gonzaga, she was the twenty-ninth sovereign of Portugal. She was born in Rio de Janeiro on 4 April 1819, the daughter of Dom Pedro IV of Portugal (Dom Pedro I of Brazil) and his wife, the Archduchess Leopoldina of Austria. Her first marriage was to Augusto de Leuchtenberg – who died young – and her second was to Dom Fernando de Saxe-Coburg-Gotha. She received the crown putatively on the abdication of her father, Dom Pedro, on condition that she should marry her uncle, Prince Miguel, at the time of the granting of the Constitutional Charter in 1826. While she was preparing to join her uncle in Vienna, he proclaimed himself absolute monarch of Portugal in a *coup d'état*, which led to the annulment of the conditions of marriage. She left for England. She defended the constitutional cause and Liberalism, travelled through Europe in 1829, at the age of just 9, forming a strong personality, at the critical moment when Portugal was going through one of the most dramatic and painful periods of its history, engaged in a violent and fratricidal civil war. She returned to Portugal in 1831, accompanied by her father. The disembarkation of the Portuguese troops at Mindelo in 1832 led to the victory of the Liberal cause, and Dona Maria was proclaimed Queen of Portugal two years later, at the age of just 15. During her reign she faced various movements and uprisings, shock waves from the Civil War, among them the insurrections of Maria da Fonte and of the Patuleia. By her second marriage she had eleven children, the first of whom was to become King Pedro V. She died giving birth to her last child, who did not survive. Only after the death of the queen did Dom Fernando II decide that the rooms normally occupied by her should pass to his personal use. With the death of Dom Fernando, and after the sale of the palace and the park to the state by the Condessa of Edla, the then Crown Prince Carlos de Bragança and his wife decided to live in Pena Palace in the summer.

DOM CARLOS I (1863–1908)

Carlos de Bragança was the grandson and protégé of Dom Fernando II. The last but one King of Portugal, Carlos I, was born in Lisbon on 28 September 1863 and died, the victim of an assault, on 1 February 1908. His full name was Carlos Fernando Luís Victor Miguel Rafael Gabriel Gonzaga Xavier Francisco de Assis José Simão, and he was baptized in the church of São Domingos in Lisbon on 19 October 1863. Dom Carlos had a full education, embracing science, arts, literature and modern languages. He was famously fond of painting and left a vast *oeuvre*. He was also interested in maritime research, becoming one of the pioneers of oceanography, in parallel with his cousin, Prince Pierre I of Monaco. He married Princess Maria Amélia de Orléans in 1886, the daughter of the Count and Countess of Paris, having come to the throne in 1889, immediately after the death of his father, King Luís I (1838–89). His reign was marked by political and social agitation in a phase of expansion of the republican movement, to which he succumbed, assassinated on the Terreiro do Paço in Lisbon, when the royal family returned from Vila Viçosa on 1 February 1908. Crown Prince Luís Filipe was also mortally wounded on this occasion.

Queen Amélia and Kaiser Wilhelm II of Germany on a visit to Pena Park on 29 March 1905, photograph by António Novaes (Photographic Archive of Lisbon Town Hall)

DONA AMÉLIA (1865-1951)

Queen Amélia was born in Twickenham (England) on 28 September 1865 and died in Versailles on 25 October 1951. She was baptized with the full name of Maria Amélia Luísa Helena. She was the daughter of the Duke and Duchess of Orléans. Her education was oriented towards the arts, modern languages, the sciences and horse riding, and she was particularly keen on drawing and painting. She married Crown Prince Carlos de Bragança on 22 May 1886 in the church of São Domingos in Lisbon. The couple went to live in the Palácio das Necessidades, and they also used the Palácio de Belém. On 21 March 1887 their first child, Prince Luís Filipe, was born in Vila Viçosa. On 14 December the following year their second child was born prematurely and died two hours later. On 15 November 1889, Prince Manuel was born. Queen Amélia dedicated herself to the Obra de Assistência dos Tuberculosos, which was founded in 1899 on her initiative. She also developed dispensaries and did countless other social and charitable works. After the assassination of the king she gave her support to her son, Manuel II, who was inexperienced and ill-prepared for the post that he was now forced to

occupy. Queen Amélia considered the Pena Palace her favourite residence. She was there when the revolution of 5 October 1910 took place, after which she left Sintra for Mafra with her mother-in-law, Queen Maria Pia. There she met her dethroned son and they left for exile from Ericeira, with the royal retinue.

DOM MANUEL II (1889-1932)

The last King of Portugal, Dom Manuel II was born in Lisbon in the Palácio de Belém, on 9 March 1889, and died in Twickenham (England) on 2 July 1932. He was baptized with the full name of Manuel Maria Filipe Carlos Amélio Luís Miguel Rafael Gonzaga Xavier Francisco de Assis Eugénio. Although he was not expected to ascend to the throne, he became King of Portugal in 1908 following the assassination of his father, Dom Carlos I and his brother Crown Prince Luís Filipe. The monarch, young and inexperienced, manifested peacemaking sentiments with sincerity. However, republican propaganda proved itself unstoppable, and the monarch embraced exile when the republic was established in Lisbon on 5 October 1910.

Above: Queen Amélia. Portrait by Vitor Corcos, signed and dated, oil on canvas, 1905 (National Coach Museum collection)

Left: Queen Amélia at Pena Palace, photograph by Atelier Fillon (Pena National Palace Collection)

ESSENTIAL BIBLIOGRAPHY

In view of the impossibility of providing an exhaustive bibliography on the subject and for more information about Dom Fernando II, a pivotal character in the history of the Pena Palace, it is absolutely indispensable to consult the excellent study by José Teixeira, *D. Fernando II, Rei-Artista, Artista-Rei*, Fundação da Casa de Bragança, Lisbon, 1986. There is a small piece on Dom Fernando (with a translation in German) in Marion Ehrhardt, *D. Fernando II – Um Mecenas Alemão Regente de Portugal*, Paisagem, Col. Paisagem-Arte, no. 7, Porto, 1985. On Pena Palace, see also, by José Martins Carneiro and Luís Marques da Gama, *Palácio Nacional da Pena – Roteiro*, Elo, Lisbon/Mafra, 1994. For further information on Portuguese revivalist architecture the exhaustive thesis of Regina Anacleto, *Arquitectura Neomedieval Portuguesa – 1780–1924*, 2 vols., Fundação Calouste Gulbenkian/ JNICT, Lisbon, 1997, is worth consulting. For the Romantic context in general and artistic creation in Portugal, the monumental work of José-Augusto França, *A Arte em Portugal no século XIX*, 2 vols., Bertrand, Lisbon, 1981, is compulsory reading.

On Sintra, there is a great deal of literature, but see the essay by Vítor Serrão, *Sintra*, Presença, Lisbon, 1989; and also the reports *Romantismo*, 3 vols., Instituto de Sintra, Sintra, 1988, with various articles by different authors, all relating to the Romantic context of the Serra de Sintra and other themes.

GENERAL BIBLIOGRAPHY

Regina Anacleto, *Arquitectura Neomedieval Portuguesa – 1780-1924*, 2 vols., Fundação Calouste Gulbenkian/JNICT, Lisboa, 1997.

Regina Anacleto, *O Neo-Manuelino ou a Reinvenção da Arquitectura dos Descobrimentos*, Catálogo, Comissão para as Comemorações dos Descobrimentos Portugueses, Lisboa, 1994.

José Martins Carneiro, *Reais Paço e Parque da Pena*, ed. CMS, Sintra, 1997.

A. Feliciano de Castilho, "O Rei Artista", in *Revista Universal*, n.º 7, 1842.

Abade de Castro e Sousa, *Memórias históricas sobre a origem da fundação do Real Mosteiro de Nossa Senhora da Pena*, 1841.

José-Augusto França, *A Arte em Portugal no século XIX*, 2 vols., Bertrand, Lisboa, 1981.

Mário Azevedo Gomes, *Monografia do Parque da Pena*, Lisboa, 1960.

Armando de Lucena, *Águas-Fortes do Rei D. Fernando*, Palácio Nacional da Pena, Sintra, 1947.

Paulo Pereira, "O revivalismo: a arquitectura do desejo", in *História da Arte em Portugal*, 3.º vol., Círculo de Leitores, Lisboa, 1995.

Paulo Pereira, *Varnhagen, historien de l'art du romantisme et le manuélin*, separata das Actas do XXVII Congresso Internacional de História de Arte, Estrasburgo, 1989.

A. Raczynski, *Dictionnaire Historico-Artistique du Portugal*, Jules Renouard et Cie., Paris, 1847.

A. Raczynski, *Les Arts en Portugal*, Jules Renouard et Cie., Paris, 1846.

Ernesto Soares, *El-Rei D. Fernando II Artista*, Fundação da Casa de Bragança, Lisboa, 1952.

M. Tude de Sousa, *Mosteiro, Palácio e Parque da Pena na Serra de Sintra*, Sintra-Gráfica, Sintra, 1951.

José Teixeira, *D. Fernando II, Rei-Artista, Artista-Rei*, Fundação da Casa de Bragança, Lisboa, 1986.

INDEX